Invisible Patterns

INVISIBLE PATTERNS

Ecology and Wisdom in Business and Profit

JON LUND HANSEN

with Per A. Christensen

Foreword by Gerhard Heiberg

Seymour Itzkoff, Imprint Adviser

Q

Quorum Books
Westport, Connecticut • London

Library of Congress Cataloging-in-Publication Data

Hansen, Jon Lund.
    Invisible patterns : ecology and wisdom in business and profit /
  Jon Lund Hansen with Per A. Christensen.
        p.   cm.
    Includes bibliographical references (p.   ) and index.
    ISBN 0–89930–916–X (alk. paper)
    1. Organizational change. 2. Problem solving. 3. Work
  environment. 4. Quality of work life. 5. Business ethics.
  I. Christensen, Per A.   II. Title.
  HD58.8.H3634   1995
  658.4—dc20   95–6922

British Library Cataloguing in Publication Data is available.

Library of Congress Catalog Card Number: 95–6922
ISBN: 0–89930–916–X

First published in 1995

Quorum Books, 88 Post Road West, Westport, CT 06881
An imprint of Greenwood Publishing Group, Inc.

Printed in the United States of America

The paper used in this book complies with the
Permanent Paper Standard issued by the National
Information Standards Organization (Z39.48–1984).

10 9 8 7 6 5 4 3 2 1

Copyright Acknowledgments

The author and publisher are grateful for permission to reproduce portions of the
following copyrighted material.

British Gas Environmental Review 1992. Quoted with permission from British Gas.

"Corporate Profile." Quoted with permission from Aracruz Celulose.

Monsanto Backgrounder brochure. Quoted with permission from Monsanto Company.

"Xerox Corporation and the Environment" brochure. Quoted with permission from Xerox
Corporation.

"Xerox: Design for the Environment," case study at Harvard Business School, prepared by
Fiona E. S. Murray. Quoted with permission from Xerox Corporation.

658.4
Han

Contents

Figures and Tables

TABLES

Foreword

Business managers today have to face more complex strategic choices than ever before. Their decision-making abilities are put to the test by internationalization, growing amounts of information, and the need for quicker decisions. At the same time, the consequences of the strategic choices are immediately visible in the reality of international competition. Both the access to new markets and the opportunities to make a profit are very good. This situation demands high ethical standards and an active choice of values on the part of the decision-makers. Both customers and the representatives of business and industry impose such demands. In this reality we need concepts and models that effectively help the decision-maker to catch the essential pattern hidden behind all the facts and details. We also need models that help us to sort our values and clarify our ethical basis for decisions.

In my work as a business manager, I have also met many internal challenges in connection with organization, motivation, and human resources management. That these areas could be enlightened by ecological theory, as the authors of this book showed me in 1989, surprised me at the time. This book makes perfectly clear that it is possible to use this theory as a basis for drawing specific conclusions and preparing guidelines for management in practice. The world has become more complex even within the individual enterprise. Demands regarding design of the work place, organization, and information processes are constantly increasing—managers have to consider the job satisfaction of their employees while still maintaining productivity at a competitive level. In fact, it is hardly possible to conceptualize the relation between people and their working environment without just this ecological perspective.

The 1994 Olympic Winter Games at Lillehammer symbolize that the days are past when people could disregard the consequences of their actions. Environmental considerations ran like a green thread throughout the whole event. To mention a few examples: (1) we gave preference to architectural solutions that caused the least wounds to nature and on the original residential environment; (2) an important criterion for selection of building materials was that they were environmentally friendly; (3) the site of a large hall for skating was changed, so that the birds in the important wetland areas could be left in peace; (4) waste sorting was practiced extensively; and (5) at all times we collaborated with important nature conservation organizations to find the best solutions.

Even in my role as Chairman of the Board in one of Europe's significant corporations I have to face these new realities. Today neither we, nor any other enterprise in the industrialized world, can neglect the environmental impacts of our activities and simultaneously regard ourselves as ethically worthy. At the same time, the environmental concerns open up for new business opportunities, new markets, and new products. From a business point of view, the challenge and inspiration in this connection lie in a sound combination of profit and protection of the environment.

The environmental problems cast their shadows before us into the next century. We are just at the beginning of the essential constructive debate on our choice of path in the future. This book provides many valuable contributions to this debate. Although I do not share all the authors' standpoints, I salute their contribution—it inspires me in the generation of my own opinions.

To me, the ecological path, as sketched here by the authors, is both inspiring and thought-provoking. I hope many decision-makers find time to read this book. And I sincerely hope that the ecological perspectives will be given their right place in our future choices—choices that we all in the end help to make.

Gerhard Heiberg
President, Lillehammer Olympic Organising Committee (LOOC)
Member of International Olympic Committee (IOC)
Chairman of the Board of Aker A/S

Acknowledgments

First of all, I would like to thank my clients for their cooperative attitude and willingness to learn along with me. I feel that our joint actions to optimize business, whether in the area of strategy implementation, productivity optimizing, or general problem solving, have been the most important basis for the project resulting in this book.

For inspiring discussions, I thank my colleagues in Business Development International (BDI): Charlie Badenhop, at ARATI K.K., Japan; Charlotte Bretto Milliner, at the Center for Professional Development, U.S.; and Judith DeLozier, at DeLozier and Associates, U.S.

I give special thanks to those who have spent time reading and criticizing this manuscript: Dipl.-Ing. Hans-Jürgen Braun, at Fraunhofer-Institut für Produktionstechnik und Automatisierung, Germany; Psychologist Tor Endestad, at the Center for Industrial Research, SINTEF, Norway; Senior Banker Odd Haugan, at the European Bank for Reconstruction and Development, London; Managing Director Finn R. Kulaas, STATOIL (U.K.) Ltd., London; Professor Torsten Malmberg, at Human Ecology Division, University of Lund, Sweden; and Jan Eystein Sæbø, Business Planner (Scandinavia) at Pepsi-Cola International, Oslo.

I would also like to thank all the corporations who generously shared their material on environmental philosophy, strategy and practice with me.

Introduction

The story goes like this: A man is searching for something on the pavement beneath the light of a street lamp. It is late at night. A policeman passes by and stops to ask what the man is searching for. The man's answer is that he is looking for the keys to his car. "And this is where you lost them?" the policeman asks. "No," the man replies. "I lost them further down the street, but it is so dark down there. I prefer to search for them here, in the light of the street lamp."

Some areas of business are elucidated, easy to identify, easy to quantify. Behind this, however, there are patterns that are hidden in darkness. This book is about these invisible patterns.

Part I, "Ecology Is the Megatrend," shows that an emerging megatrend as we move toward the next century is ecology, a trend that holds huge potentials for profit in new areas. I also introduce some key concepts to be applied all throughout the book. The basic aspects of natural ecosystems are presented, and an overview of organizational ecology in general is also given.

Part II, "Organizations as Ecosystems," discloses the invisible patterns of human systems. The natural ecosystem is chosen as metaphor, and real-life examples from organizational contexts show how this applies to business. A whole new theory of resistance to organizational change is presented, together with practical prescriptions for turning resistance into a constructive force.

Part III, "Ancient Man in Modern Organizations," shows the similarities between ancient man and modern industrial man. Most theorists of management and organization wrongly perceive man's behavior as wholly rational. But this is an inadequate conception, as man's deeper, biological layers should be considered. The implications of this perspective for leadership, change, organizing, work place design, and problem solving are shown.

Part IV, "Organizational Ecology and Strategic Leadership," shows how the premises of the book so far build up to a model where organizational ecology is linked to strategic leadership. This model is presented in more detail and is exemplified.

Part V, "The Ecological Path," further elaborates the new megatrend of ecology. The need for sound, ecological change and development is discussed, as well as an overall ecological worldview. The role of business is discussed, and business ethics in our days of ecological crisis highlighted.

Part VI, "Profits, Ethics, and Eco-Problems," discusses ethical limitations and business opportunities in the age of ecology. The "greening" of business is mainstream, but ecology has much wider implications. A comprehensive factor for ecological contributions in business is presented and exemplified.

I recommend that the chapters and parts be read in the same order as they appear, since each chapter builds on the ones preceding it.

Industrial man lost his keys to sound development some generations ago, and ever since he has been searching under the street lights of technology and economy. But the keys are to be found in the darkness of ecology, with all its implications for the fundamental questions of values, ethics, and life quality, and for profitability, good leadership, and organizational understanding. I invite you to join me in the further search for these invisible patterns.

Part I

Ecology Is the Megatrend

[T]he ideas which dominate our civilization at the present time, in their most virulent form stem from the Industrial Revolution. They may be summarized as: (a) It's us *against* the environment, (b) It's us *against* other men, (c) It's the individual (or the individual company, or the individual nation) that matters.... We submit that these ideas are simply proved false by the great but ultimately destructive achievements of our technology in the last 150 years. Likewise, they appear to be false under modern ecological theory. *The creature that wins against its environment destroys itself.*

Gregory Bateson, *Steps to an Ecology of Mind*

Chapter 1

The New Megatrend

> We must learn from nature's complicated mechanism, of which we still are a part. We must let this learning be our guide in all aspects of our life, privately as well as in the management of our society.
> Thor Heyerdahl, Foreword to Hansen et al., *Broad Ecology*
> [author's translation]

Ecology originally was the domain of biologists. It labeled the part of biology that describes how living organisms interact with and adapt to their environment. It also came to include the relationships between organisms. Then human ecology was added. Today, ecology is a cross-disciplinary perspective where physicians, economists, sociologists, biologists, anthropologists, philosophers, and many others join forces. The aims are the improvement of man's life on earth, the protection of the global ecosystems with all their species, and the scientific understanding of all organisms—their physiology, behavior, and relationships.

We are now experiencing an ecological movement of such dimensions that the tag "megatrend" is appropriate. Today we can hardly open a newspaper or periodical without finding reports on environmental or ecological issues. Schoolchildren challenge their parents' buying behavior, craving environmentally friendly choices of products; television programs educate us all in ecological thinking; business partners investigate each other's environmental practices and demand convincing annual reports on their treatment of the environment. Bookstores bulge with new literature on ecology and science, ecological aspects of architecture, and ecology and business, to mention only a few.

The international market for environmental technology in 1993 was estimated at $200 billion.[1] Along with this comes the niche of direct waste management. The largest waste management company in Europe in 1991 sold for $1.2 billion; the five largest companies together sold for $3.9 billion.[2] Private and public activities cleaning the environment and improving it must be added. There is no doubt that the direct environmental market is growing fast and contains some of the most profitable and safe niches for investment in business today.

At the same time, an environmentally friendly turnaround of existing business is happening on a large scale, primarily by lowering energy and raw material consumption and minimizing pollution and waste, and through recycling and cradle-to-grave strategies for products. For instance, 3M was a pioneer in the field with its 1975 3P program (Pollution Prevention Pays). Their results: more than 600,000 tons of pollution prevented and more than $570 million saved (in terms of cumulative first-year savings) from 1975 to 1992.[3] Now nearly all of the large corporations are "going green," and a lot of the smaller ones, too. Volkswagen, Opel, Toyota, IBM, Johnson & Johnson, Dow, Xerox, Canon, British Airways, Scandinavian Airlines, Lufthansa, BP, Exxon, Shell, Pepsi Cola, Coca-Cola, McDonald's, AT&T, Eastman Kodak, Siemens, Electrolux—all of these are doing it, and thousands of others are following suit.

ICI, for one, carried an expenditure on the environment of 300 million pounds sterling in 1992. The same year Kodak donated $2.5 million to the World Wildlife Fund for an environmental education initiative, "Windows on the Wild." In 1991, Dow spent $231 million on environmental capital projects.[4] This certainly places a significant price tag on green profiling. But it is worth it. The greening of business is a fact—consumers love it, and profits go up!

The other side of the coin shows the possible fallacies of *not* greening fast enough. Although a disappointment to the most eager environmentalists, the Rio Conference in June 1992, with its tremendous participation by organizations and the media, signaled that the laying down of international regulations and national laws may take on speed and place heavier restrictions on business in many areas. The businesses that lag behind will be punished, both directly by the legislation and indirectly by the market.

Several surveys have shown that the market is interested. For example, from 1986 to 1991 there was a 100% increase (i.e., from 35% in 1986 to 70% in 1991) in consumers in the United States who said that recyclability affected their choice of products.[5] Membership in environmental organizations is booming. In the United States, Greenpeace grew from 6,000 members in 1970 to two million in 1990. Membership in the Worldwide Fund for Nature in England grew from 12,000 in 1971 to 231,000 in 1990.[6] These are typical figures.

A 1989 public poll in Europe revealed that the protection of the environment ranked second only to unemployment as the most important political issue facing the European Community. Fifty-three percent of French, German and British respondents stated that they would buy a product less harmful to the environment even if it cost more (McCann Erikson Harris Research Center, 1990). A little later, a 1991 Gallup poll showed that 76% of all Americans considered themselves environmentalists and a 1992 Roper poll indicated that 78% of the American public felt that the government should take action on environmental issues right away.[7]

The potential for both direct savings in production and for winning market shares by going green is obvious and well documented.[8]

Lifestyles are changing, and will change even more in times to come, as a part of the growing green consciousness. People are searching, and will search even more in the future for nonmaterial values as annihilation spreads in the industrialized world. This expands old markets and opens up new ones. People in the industrialized world are attracted by art and culture more than before. For example, from 1970 to 1990, opera audiences in the United States nearly tripled. From 1965 to 1990, attendance at U.S. museums rose from 200 to 500 million.[9] Another trend is the "alternative" wave, covering everything from extrasensory perception to acupuncture, from yoga to martial arts and tea sermons to biodynamic agriculture. Many well-off people in the industrialized world are searching for meaning and identity; there is a tremendous market. Ecology already represents a significant factor in fashion. "Eco-style," "eco-like," "the eco-way"—it already is there in clothing, soft drinks, weeklies, and cafes.

The new ecological consciousness has implications for all business niches. Let us take as an example the fastest growing market of all, tourism: 10.6% of the total global work force is employed in the travel and tourism sector. John Naisbitt says: "Travel and tourism will create 144 million jobs worldwide between now and the year 2005—112 million in fast-growing Asia Pacific."[10] What is the connection between the growing ecological consciousness and tourism? On the one hand, tourism and travel represent a heavy stress on the environment, and a threat to local culture. What does mass tourism do to Spain, for example, which receives 35.3 million tourists every year, and has a population of about 39 million, or to Greece, with 8 million tourists, itself containing a population of about 10 million (1991 numbers)?[11] Mass tourism causes large-scale cultural and physiochemical environmental problems. For this reason, the new ecological consciousness could put a brake on its development. At the same time, tourism could take on new "ecological" characteristics: Traditional mass tourism could fade and be replaced by new forms. We already see a growing interest in tourism with a more authentic content, and also the emerging niche of "eco-tourism." And if John Naisbitt is right in his prediction of a world of a thousand countries, with strong and authentic local cultures, tourism may become a more differentiated and valuable activity, different from the mass tourism we now know.[12]

What general implications does the megatrend of ecology have for the global market for raw materials and products? Ideally, it should imply negative economic growth in the rich countries, and/or a shift in consumption from goods (high environmental costs) to services (generally lower environmental costs). It also should imply a reduction in international trade (high environmental costs) and a general strengthening of the superordinate ecological principle of *local production for local consumption for local recirculation.*[13]

How do other factors fit into this picture? On the one hand, we see a tendency toward even stronger division of labor among countries. The competitive advantage for mass production in countries with cheap labor should move traditional mass-producing factories to these areas. Some Japanese companies, among others, demonstrate this trend by moving mass production of television sets, video recorders, and cameras to Malaysia, China, and the Philippines. The competitive advantage of high-tech knowledge should attract specialized production to the countries possessing such expertise. Potential competitive advantage may further enhance international work sharing, leaving some countries to specialize in agriculture, others in fishery, still others in forestry, electronics, automobiles, tourism, and so on.

On the other hand, transport of raw materials and products entails both economic and environmental costs. The pressure of environmentalism may well cause a development away from trade with material goods. This development will also be strengthened by a need for closeness to the market, to satisfy local needs and to maintain flexibility. Again some Japanese corporations illustrate this. Nissan moved the manufacture of some models to England, Toyota to the United States. The gain is closeness to the market, doing away with trade barriers, and achieving a local standing in the marketplace.

"How is it possible," asks Paul Kennedy, "for a country [Japan] so dependent upon exports to be assured of continued access to important global markets, especially if its own success in industry, science, and technology threatens to make redundant the need for foreign produce?"[14]

Peter F. Drucker says: "Yet in an investment-led world economy, a strategy based on exports is out of date. One of the factors that lost the United Kingdom its economic leadership in the nineteenth century was, ironically, its mastery of exporting. . . . Since they could not penetrate their key markets by the traditional route of exports, U.S. and West German companies were obliged to establish factories there instead. They had to invest before they could trade."[15] A shift from commodity trade to export and import of finances and competence may occur. Drucker also mentions the importance of proximity to markets, market presence, and market standing. He even goes so far as to state, on a general basis, that "... a company cannot hold a leadership position in a key market unless it manufactures there."[16]

John Naisbitt, in his last "Megatrend" book, *Global Paradox*, says:

We are moving towards a world of 1,000 countries because:
   —Many people of the new tribalism want self-rule and every day they see others getting self-rule, or moving towards it.
   —The nation-state is dead. Not because nation-states were subsumed by super-states, but because they are breaking up into smaller, more efficient parts—just like big companies.
   —The revolution in telecommunications not only informs this tremendous move to democratic self-rule but monitors and makes transparent the character and nature of the process. Modern telecommunications also allow and encourage extraordinary cooperation among people, companies, and countries.[17]

Information is becoming cheaper, faster, and more all-compassing. The latest prospect, launched by Microsoft and McCaw, of a global communication network facility composed of 840 satellites, should cover 95% of the globe at all times. This may never become a reality, but something like it will. This has two implications:

First, people all over the world change as they obtain access to information. The power structures will change as people's degree of education and general knowledge of the state of affairs in the world grow. The general demand to be able to influence one's own situation, by employees, customers, the general marketplace, and the society, will grow stronger. This indicates a shift away from authoritarian, centralized leadership in business and in society. The fall of the communist regimes in the former Soviet Union and East European countries is the strongest expression of this trend. Another implication is that global education in ecology and environmentalism will speed up and be all-encompassing, further strengthening the ecological megatrend.

Second, modern communication facilities make it easier for corporations to decentralize. This further facilitates locally based production, since the physical distance to headquarters and owners becomes less relevant. This will in turn strengthen a pattern of local production for local consumption for local recirculation.

I maintain that the trend of growing ecological consciousness, together with the factors mentioned above, may imply a *decrease* in international trade of material goods, an *increase* in internationalization of know-how, information, and capital, and a strengthening of the principle of local production for local consumption for local recirculation (of material goods). The main reasons are already stated, but let us add one more thing. Will the ecological megatrend imply higher transport costs? It could. If the price of the cost of damaged nature was added, oil prices would rise further to new levels, followed by dramatic increases in transport costs. However unrealistic such dramatic changes, the possible general trend should be considered. The principle of "paying the real price" might emerge quickly, since it has strong proponents among both economists and environmentalists.[18] This would imply that a business would pay for damaging soil, woods, air, and water, maybe even pay for the side effects in the biological and social system of its activity. (The price of oil would rise many times over if the oil companies were to pay all military activities that secured their transport and all alert measures.) This would be a tremendous change from today, when the costs are carried by the commons and the profit is taken by the individual company.

The future-oriented and ecologically sound corporation should then see the world as one marketplace for information, know-how, capital and services, and as a diversity of local markets for commodities.

So far, implications of ecology for the strategic areas of finance, market, sales, and R&D (Research and Development) should be implicit in what is said. But this is not all. Ecology is not only a question of preserving the physiochemical environment. Ecology, as I present it here, implies a new worldview. For business, it has implications for organization, management, and HR (Human Resources) as well. "Environmental management needs state-of-the-art management tools to manage complexity," says Ulrich Steger at the European Business School in Germany.[19] "All hands on deck," Tom Peters says, "Environmental concerns should cross functional borders inside a firm."[20] Good leadership is profitable, competent management pays. The new trends of network organizing, delayering, delegation, and self-directed teams are all linked with the new ecological consciousness. It seems as if ecology, as has been the case with productivity, quality, and technology, should now be a cross-functional strategic focus for business in the years to come (see Figure 1.1).

For many years now, a possible shift of paradigm in science and thinking has been discussed. The change is taking place right now. A whole world is searching for lasting values, new scientific paradigms, a meaningful life, a new world order, an integration of the new information technology with the eternal values of human life. A whole world is in the process of comprehending that we all are passengers on the spaceship earth, that it has a limited amount of resources and that there is a limit to what it can endure, that we are responsible for an unending succession of generations to follow us, that everything is interconnected in the ecosystems, and that we must join forces to solve problems mankind never has faced before. This is the heaviest part of the new, ecological megatrend: About five

Figure 1.1
Areas of Activity of Potential Relevance to Business Strategy

	Economy & Finance	Marketing & Sales	Human Resources & Management	Organization	Research & Development	Other
Productivity	?	?	?	?	?	?
Quality	?	?	?	?	?	?
Technology	?	?	?	?	?	?
Ecology	Yes	Yes	Yes	Yes	Yes	Yes

billion people slowly changing their thinking and behavior along ecological lines.

Summary of the main elements of the ecological megatrend:

—The new paradigm of ecology will gain an even stronger position worldwide

—Green consciousness in the market will further increase

—Green regulations from governments worldwide will increase in number and rigor

—The market for green technology, waste management, and restoration of nature will increase

—New markets will emerge for a meaningful and better life in the rich world

—Competition to be greenest in business will increase in all industries

—Local production for local consumption for local recirculation will spread

—The ecological megatrend will mark all business niches

—One open world market for economy, information, technology, and know-how

—Strengthening of local communities and countries

—Business will decentralize, network organize, and delegate authority to local entities

—The management trend will be management by delegation and empowering.

CHECK YOURSELF: HOW WELL UPDATED ARE YOU?

• What is the status of greenery among your competitors compared to yourself?

• In which way are products/ services in your industry greening?

• What new business opportunities are emerging in your industry for a future with growing ecological consciousness?

• What is the attitude toward greening among your customers and in your potential market?

• What is the relevant legislation on the environment in your industry?

• What is the attitude toward greening in your board of directors, and among the managers and employees?

Chapter 2

Concepts of Help

Chuang said: "See how busy the trouts are. They are happy today."
Hui answered: "You are no trout. How then can you know that they
are happy?" Chuang said: "You are not me. How then can you know
that I do not know that they are happy?"

Chuang Tzu, from "The Fishes' Happiness," in Aage Marcus,
The Blue Dragon [author's translation]

A set of concepts will be used consistently throughout this book. In this
chapter they are presented and illustrated.

PUNCTUATION AND FILTERS

The scope of this book is ecology and business. This might or might not
reflect that there is an objective need for such a book, but clearly it mirrors
my belief that it is a unit of interest, for me as well as the readers. I, the
author, have made a *punctuation*, Gregory Bateson would have stated.[1]
Out of the universe of all things, this happens to be my focus point. What
the concept of punctuation signifies is that any description implies a de-
limitation in time and space. For example, when developing strategies in
business, a certain time frame is punctuated for visions, goals, and objectives. When strategic objectives are developed, certain focus areas are
punctuated, implying a punctuation in space. For obvious reasons we are
unable to perceive "everything." The perception of "everything" is for
mystics, not for scientists or businessmen.

Any description is a description, not reality itself. This goes even for "objective phenomena." For example, the psychology of witnesses who have attended exactly the same event simultaneously has shown conclusively that what is described varies surprisingly. Even more relative is the world of "good and bad." An ancient Norwegian folktale tells about the rabbit that had been married. Exploding with joy he comes jumping and running over the field. He meets a fox. The rabbit exclaims: "This is my lucky day, you should know, because I have been married." "That is a good thing," the fox said. "Not that good, she was a miser and a witch," the rabbit said. "That was bad," the fox said. "Not that bad really," the rabbit said, "as she was rich and owned a house." "That was good," the fox said. "Not that good, really," the rabbit said, "the house burnt down, and all our properties with it." "That is very sad!" said the fox. "Not that sad, really, as my wife burnt with it!" the rabbit exclaimed, jumping and singing further over the field.

Further understanding may be reached by the concept of *filters*.[2] Imagine that you look at the world through spectacles. If they are colored red, you see a red world out there. Your filter is then red. Imagine that looking through your own concepts and sensory apparatus implies filtering the world. We can never see it as it "really" is, only the way our biological sensory apparatus, together with cultural and individual learning, makes us see it. Walking through the streets of London an architect may see the colors and shapes of the buildings and see different styles and examples of periods. A social worker might see these same things as reflections of class and living standards, whereas an economist sees the business potentials of different locations and buildings.

Differences of punctuation and filters all too often are perceived as disagreements. But "real" disagreements are more rare. For instance, a discussion of marketing strategy for a certain product is taken in the management group. The director of finance may focus on a cost-benefit aspect of the case in the short run. The marketing director may focus on the long-term importance of the product as a market opener for other products to follow. The manager of logistics may focus on the capacity of the back-up apparatus to handle it all, and to the service manager the relevant aspect is the competence level of the service personnel. They can all be right, but represent different punctuations and filters. Agreement may eventually be reached when a common evaluation is made of all aspects in relation to the whole business.

The concepts of punctuation and filters are of great help in enhancing understanding of differing viewpoints. Not the least, they are helpful when we try to understand ourselves. It has been said: "To understand the world you must first understand yourself."

Figure 2.1
The Four Mental Positions

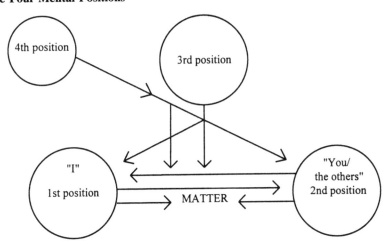

MENTAL POSITIONS

By mental position, I refer to the fact that we share the ability to see a matter or an issue from different angles. We can shift around, and understand our own and other people's points of view. To structure it:

Overview of four mental positions:

First position: The matter is perceived and understood from one's own point of view and out of consideration for one's "own interests."

Second position: The matter is perceived and understood from the other's point of view and out of consideration for his "own interests."

Third position: The matter is perceived and understood from an outside viewpoint and is based on the common interests of the system as a whole.

Fourth position: The perception of one's own values and punctuation in all positions (see Figure 2.1).

A strategy meeting in the top management team discusses competition and prices. The conclusion is clear: A lowering of prices will increase market shares considerably. After this the next step will be to introduce high-margin products to the customers, and thereafter stabilize prices and market. The decision is made, and the strategy fails. Why?

The team has left important perspectives out of the discussion, only relying on one—their own, their first position.[3] The basis was their own interests, beliefs, their own sense of logic. From this perspective the decision was clear and intelligent. But how would the competitors respond? What would *they* receive of information, what would they feel, think, and do? These questions were never asked. If the management team had tried a second position view, specifically the competitor's view, the following would have emerged as the most probable consideration on the part of the competitors: "They are lowering prices, obviously to win market shares. Okay, let's see if we can beat them. We lower the prices of our common products even more, and inform the market through an extensive advertisement campaign?" It would have been wise to check out the second position before reaching a conclusion.

But what about the *interaction* between the "us" and "them?" Seeing this would have implied taking a third position. This might have led to still another understanding: From this perspective it might have been possible to envisage the potential escalation of a price war.

From the first position one is tempted to go for win-lose (we win, they lose) strategies which, from a third position point of view, are obvious lose-lose strategies. From an ecological point of view, win-lose strategies are obvious losing strategies: As everything is interconnected and mutually dependent, if you lose, I lose. The ecological view tends to punctuate larger units of time and space. With that punctuation the mutual losses of win-lose strategies are more easily perceived.

Even in the third position we see through our subjective filters, make our punctuation, and bring our presuppositions with us. The third position is not identical with "neutrality" or "objectivity." The point of view that reflects this and understands that in any case (be it seen from first, second, or third position) my evaluation is based on a set of values, patterns of thinking, and a selected amount of data, I call fourth position. The underlying notions of the management team starting the price war could be, for example, "It's a good thing to beat one's competitors." "One man's meat is another man's poison." "Down-pricing is an effective means of winning market shares." "Higher market shares bring more profit in the long run, which is good." Applying the fourth position, they could have questioned these presuppositions.

In this way I have criticized our imagined top management team in the example above for only taking a first position. Their punctuation also might have been too narrow, for example, "gross turnover next quarter in market segment X." A broader punctuation, like "our profitability in relation to the whole market for the next five years," could have been of help and might have led to other conclusions.

HIERARCHIES

To make a complex world a little easier to handle, we sort it hierarchically. The zoologist groups species, psychologists sort human motives, decision makers construct priority hierarchies, sociologists define aggregates of populations and community levels. When the medals are handed over after a sports event, the gold winner is at the top, the silver and bronze winners below, forming a pyramid. Organizational maps, at least of line organizations, usually have the shape of a pyramid, and man is often placed at the top of the pyramid of the animal kingdom. It is of importance to remember that these constructions are not reality, they are aids in sorting and rationalizing reality.

A common misconception is that "what is at the top has the highest value." But that only goes for a *value hierarchy*! In an organizational hierarchy, the most valuable person may be an irreplaceable researcher down in the R&D department. Or, as some businesses think: "The most valuable persons are the ones closest to our customers." In the context of taking on spans of responsibilities, the organization's map often gives a fairly accurate picture. The broadest span of responsibilities corresponds to the top level, and narrower spans follow downward. Wages correlate to a high degree with this map. This should again not be confused, however, with the value of the private person. The wage is the price of the function or the performance, not the person.

Biologists construct food pyramids, with predators, like man, at the top, over the consumers of plants and the plants themselves. This is not a value hierarchy. If a hierarchy were to be constructed of the most irreplaceable species in the ecosystems, man would have to be placed far down! If species were sorted by size of brain, man would be beneath the elephant. If the sorting is by ability to exploit nature, develop technology, handle third and fourth position, and kill members of its own species, man is at the top! Still, this is not a value hierarchy.

A less widely known feature of some hierarchies, called "logical levels," appears when we approach it strictly formally (see Figure 2.2). I call this a *hierarchy of logical levels*.[4] We can say that any level of this formal structure signifies a class, the members of the class appearing on the next lower level. For example, the class "land mammals" contains members like "humans," "chimpanzees," "goats," "tigers," and so on. This strict logical taxonomy is typical of maps of species in biology. Thus, asking "what is an example of X?" typically gives an answer at a lower logical level than X. There are always more cases on the lower levels. If man were the only land mammal, class and member would be identical. But then no good reason for making it a class would exist. We can thus state this rule: *There is always more than one member of a class.* A business strategy has a structure that also may be visualized hierarchically (see Figure 2.3).

What significance does this have? Look at Figure 2.3 again. The structure of a business strategy can also be seen as a hierarchy of means and ends. Objectives are ends in relation to actions. But in relation to goals they are means. Goals are ends in relation to objectives, but means in relation to the vision. Whether something constitutes a means or an end depends then on the punctuation you make. And nothing is a means or

Figure 2.2
The Structure of a Hierarchy of Logical Levels

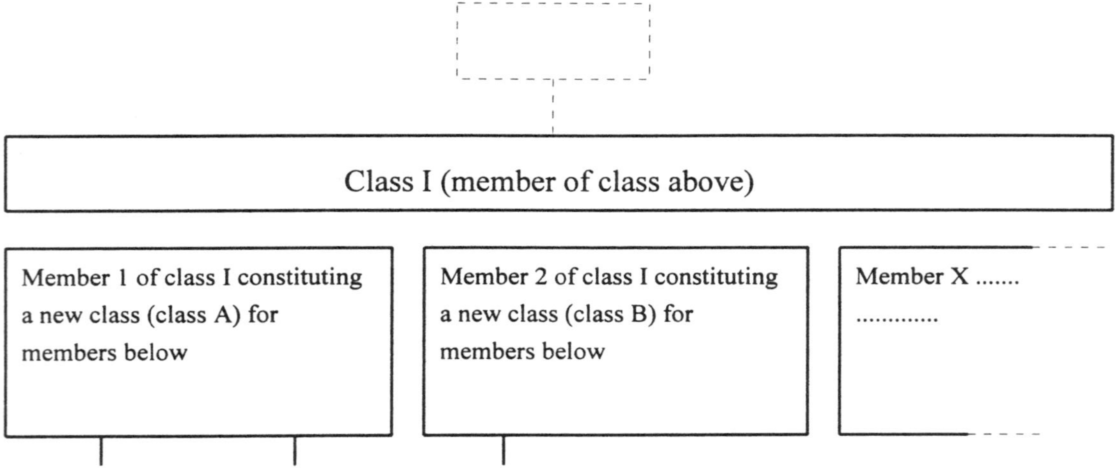

Class I (member of class above)

Member 1 of class I constituting a new class (class A) for members below

Member 2 of class I constituting a new class (class B) for members below

Member X ....
....

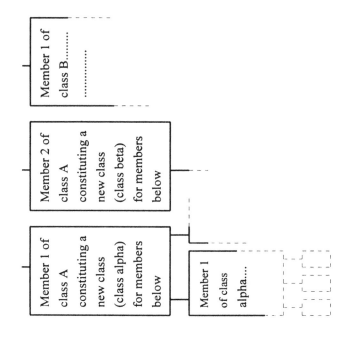

Figure 2.3
The Logical Structure of the Dynamic Elements of a Business Strategy

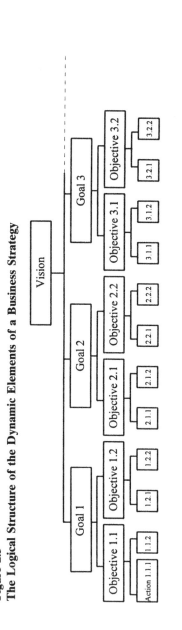

an end in and by itself, only in relation to other elements. The further you push this upward, the closer to questions of value and meaning you come. A phrasing like "what would be the outcome of this" moves you through objectives to goals and through goals to vision.

We now can broaden our rule that there is always more than one member of the class, to *there is always more than one means to an end*. There is always more than one possible set of goals leading to the vision, more than one set of possible objectives leading to the goals, and more than one set of possible actions leading to the fulfillment of the objectives. This opens for choice. Let us take an example. The idea of global economic growth to solve environmental problems can be seen as an end. This closes for choice. If we split it, and label solving the environmental problems as the end, then global economic growth can be seen as one of many possible means to this end.

The activity in some business niches is obviously particularly threatening to the environment. The big oil companies' activities could serve as an example, implying as they do risky production and freight, and in the end increased emissions of carbon dioxide. Is oil exploitation to be seen as means or end? If we see it as means, what is the end? The end could be making large amounts of energy available. Other means than oil exploitation to that end would be the development of solar technology, coal mining, building of nuclear reactors, and so on.

What happens when we go further up in this hierarchical structure of means and ends? (See Figure 2.4). We see that oil exploitation is a means, of many, to achieve certain ends. The further up we move, the more means appear on the lower levels. There obviously are a whole lot of alternatives to oil production to bring about a better future for mankind! What if we take the oil companys' first position? Another hierarchy of logical levels would appear (Figure 2.5). The lesson this teaches us is this: Nothing is an end in itself independent of position. There is always a choice. One choice on a certain level implies a whole set of choices across levels, and always implies values. Our punctuation differs, and with it our conclusions.

The *hierarchy of system levels* consists of larger and larger punctuation upward in the hierarchy. For example, man may be studied as an individual, a family member, a member of a community or in the frame of society at large. According to hierarchy theory, the larger units set the conditions for the smaller. A family's choices will depend on the culture, economy, and technology of society at large. Persons acting "normally" in a mental hospital for psychotics may be diagnosed as schizophrenic, because their individual normality in the context of insanity is insane. Good deeds from one of the partners of a marriage in crisis may enhance crisis, because in the context it is perceived as hidden hostility.

When discussing strategies for ecological change, this is of utmost importance. We should always check the conditions laid down by the higher

Figure 2.4
The Means and Ends of Energy Exploitation in a Logical Structure

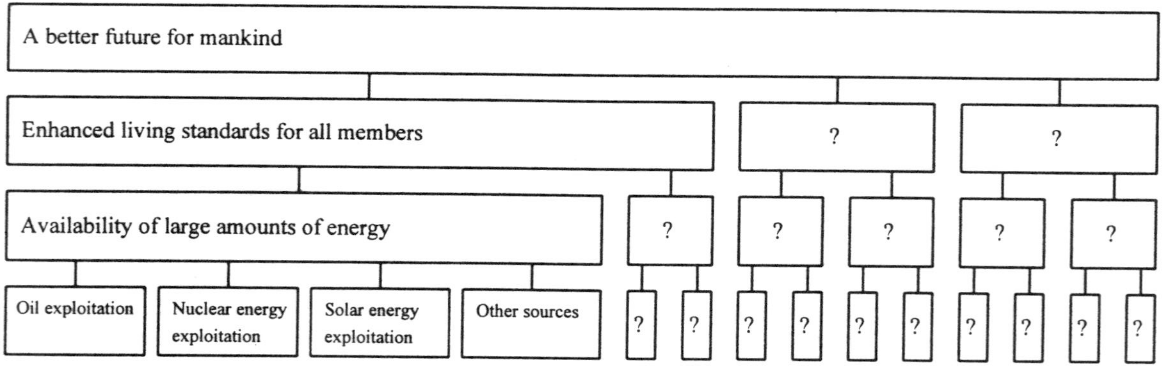

Figure 2.5
The Means and Ends of Oil Exploitation as Seen from First Position

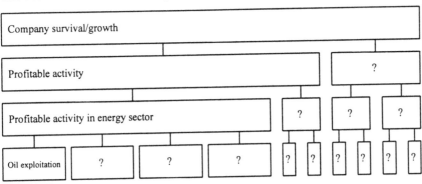

levels in the hierarchy, inside which our actions are intended to give results. Single-department developments in corporations often cause sur-
prises. A positive result may be neutralized, or even turned to the
negative, because of the overruling conditions set by the larger system, as
in this example:

A quality-enhancement program in the service department of a sales
organization proceeded very favorably for some months. Then resistance
emerged from other departments. The project was defined as time wasted
in the very result-oriented culture of the enterprise. The results of the
project turned to the negative and interdepartmental conflicts arose. The
higher system levels set conditions that had not been complied with in the
service department (Figure 2.6).

THREE TYPES OF CHANGE-PROCESSES

This book will talk a lot about change and change-processes. What is
meant by change is ambiguous, however. It should usually refer to something more dramatic than development and adaptation, and something
more proactive than readjustment. Of interest are also the positive con-
notations the word has attained. Industrial man tends to see change as a
basic human trait, not as a cultural phenomenon. But there is every reason
to doubt this as a general truth. Change now seems to be inevitable, but
this does not imply any values in and by itself. I prefer to see change as
a means, not an end. There is no doubt, however, that changes are necessary in a changing environment. Also, no doubt should remain that the
change processes in business are the keys to success or failure in a competitive environment. How should these processes take place? Authoritarian or democratic, directive or supportive? A good conceptualization is
essential as a basis for good choices.

Figure 2.6
Example of a Hierarchy of System Levels. The higher levels set conditions for lower levels.

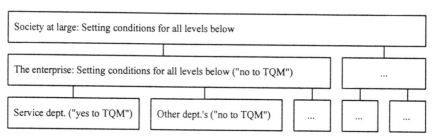

To sort the field of change-processes, I have defined three logically different categories.[5]

Overview of three categories of change-process:

1st order change-process: An action is changed by replacing it with a given alternative.

2nd order change-process: An action is changed by the person responsible for the action choosing from a set of given alternatives.

3rd order change-process: An action is changed as a result of insight into the purpose of the action. The person carrying out the action generates the alternatives, and chooses between them himself.

Let us exemplify the categories, and imagine a CEO (Chief Executive Officer) applying a 1st order change-process in his management practice: He instructs the top management group in minute detail. He gathers information, develops strategy plans on his own, and then directs the top management group on what activities they are to put into effect, together with timing and reporting details.

Example of a 2nd order change-process: The CEO gathers information himself and develops some possible strategic scenarios, as well as some possible strategic alternatives. The top management group then convenes to evaluate and decide on the alternatives to be put into effect, together with timing and reporting details.

Applying a 3rd order change-process, the CEO delegates some of the preparations for a meeting on strategy to members of the top management group. The group collectively develops the company strategy through dialogues held during the preparations and at the strategy meeting itself. Timing and reporting are collectively decided.

The implications of, and preconditions for, the differing processes, their use, and consequences will be elaborated on in Chapter 18. For now, it suffices to say that, from an ideal point of view, 3rd order change-processes are "best." With enhanced education and democratic practice, 3rd order processes will make their way to an ever-higher degree into business and society in general. It will be a must for managers of the future to understand the difference between these categories of change-processes, to understand the preconditions for, and the gains and losses of, the three respective processes in differing contexts.

CHECK YOURSELF: MANAGEMENT WITH INSIGHT

- How often do you analyze the long-term impacts of your decisions?
- How often do you analyze the impacts of your decisions on the larger system?
- How well do you understand that other people's reasoning is not "wrong" or "stupid," but quite to the contrary that it is logical, seen from second position?
- How easily do you see an interaction between others and yourself from the outside?
- How well do you know your own implicit values and filters in any evaluation or decision making?
- How well do you separate means and ends?
- How often do you clearly identify the objectives for actions under discussion?
- How often do you analyze whether the conditions at higher system levels are contrary to a decision being made?
- How conscious are you of your choice of 1st, 2nd, or 3rd order processes?
- Are you personally competent to vary between 1st, 2nd, or 3rd order processes?
- Are you conscious of whether your typical management style is management by 1st, 2nd, or 3rd order processes?

Chapter 3

A Brief Lesson on Ecosystems

We social scientists would do well to hold back our eagerness to control that world which we so imperfectly understand.... Rather, our studies could be inspired by a more ancient, but today less honored, motive: a curiosity about the world of which we are a part. The rewards of such work are not power but beauty.

Gregory Bateson, *Steps to an Ecology of Mind*

All through this book, ecology is our reference. This chapter gives a popular introduction to the ecosystem. Special emphasis is placed on the underlying patterns and laws governing the system, in themselves invisible and intangible, but all the more important.

The study of ecosystems is not only a scientific practice. It is an exercise in third position thinking. The world of simple causality has to be left behind, as well as mechanistic metaphors in general. Linear statistics are of little help, and you cannot even trust your own senses, since most of what is going on cannot be directly sensed. Macroeconomies represent a parallel: Who has ever *seen* inflation and depression? We can only see their consequences, and then deduce what is happening.

Ecosystems are complex and dynamic systems, hard to comprehend and even harder to predict. In fact, many of the underlying patterns emerge only *after* an influence is launched into the system. The wide-ranging effects of pesticides could hardly be predicted when they were first introduced. Likewise, the undesirable social and cultural effects of industrializing traditional communities could hardly have been foreseen.

Most studies of ecosystems stress the physiochemical aspects. These studies show how matter and energy are distributed and circulated through food chains, or food webs. It has also been common to describe these as hierarchies, where the green plants, or primary producers, constitute the lowest level. The next level is the plant eaters, the primary consumers. The top level is constituted by the predators, the meat eaters. When matter is handed over from organism to organism in the food web, energy is lost. One implication is that human beings can live on the grain production of a certain area that has to be fifteen times larger if the production first is to pass through a primary consumer, for example, cows. The link between top and bottom is constituted by the decomposers, that is, bacteria and fungi that split dead organisms down to the basic "building blocks" again. In fact, a circle is more illustrative of this than a pyramid. The saying from the bible, "earth to earth, ashes to ashes, dust to dust" is an accurate description of the cycle, or circulatory system, of matter in an ecosystem. To state it differently: Without death life is not possible. The two are made one in the cycle. From this point of view the enormous amount of research being done to defeat death and make life last longer seems to be a paradox.

Of special interest to us here is the fact that Mother Nature in general practices a principle already mentioned above: local production for local consumption for local recirculation. Natural systems are built up of billions of "home industries." The only deviance of significance is represented by the big circulatory systems, that is, the circulation of water and gas across systems. All ecosystems, and the sum of them, the biosphere, have one source of energy, the sun. All energy circulating in any form in the systems is a transformed form of solar energy.

An ecosystem, then, is a mainly self-sufficient and closed system. It also is an efficient production system that can hardly be simulated. Everything is used in the natural system. This does not mean that the undisturbed system has a *maximum* production (of bio-mass), but that nature's production processes are of a surprisingly economic kind. There is no unnecessary spill of energy. Nature is like a humble person who lays by, never spending more than he saves. This is a striking contrast to industrial production. In fact, economic and industrial growth in the perspective of Mother Nature's position is not growth at all. It is an expression of a situation where we take ever more from the bank for spending, and lay nothing by. Or, as Georgescu-Roegen states: "In entropy terms, the cost of any biological or economical enterprise is always greater than the product. In entropy terms, any such activity necessarily results in a deficit . . . every time we produce a Cadillac, we do it at the cost of decreasing the number of human lives in the future."[1]

The Swedish biochemist Staffan Delin uses this parable for the situation: Mother Nature's production is like a bricklayer building a house. He carefully places each brick in the right place and thereby easily builds a house with little use of energy and trash. Modern man would make big piles of bricks. He would place explosives under the piles and fire off detonations. Every now and then, by statistical chance, a brick would hit its place. After a time the house would be built, but tremendous amounts of explosives and bricks would have been spent, and the trash would be much more than the goods. The loss of energy in nature's production is close to none; the loss of energy in modern production is enormous.[2] The so-called "value creation" then is "value spending," Mother Nature might think.

There is every reason to say that nature and its production methods are close to perfect, from a theoretical biochemical point of view. Also, traditional agriculture, as it was practiced in the third and fourth worlds before the green revolution, was based on an accumulated wisdom invisible to industrial man. Punctuating a picture only covering the profitable parts, such as the production of seeds, he lost sight of the whole. The HYV (High Yielding Variety) sorts in fact are not high yielding at all. Under natural conditions they are mainly low yielding. But they have a high capacity for extra absorption of fertilizers and water, and thereby potentially can produce more food for man. But the whole picture should include all costs: dependency on fertilizers, artificial irrigation, pesticides, and production of seed grain. And, as experience with the green revolution in many places shows, the costs also should cover unemployment, hunger, degradation of soil, lack of water, acidation of soil and desertification, and breakdown of social institutions and social stability.[3] From nature's point of view, the most productive way is to build by hand, plough with oxen, eat natural food, and travel by horse.

This should not be read either as an argument for redeveloping industrial man's way of life back into a primitive form or as an argument for vegetarianism. It is a reminder of our filters. From industrial man's first position we see something that is different from what we, from a second position, could imagine as being Mother Nature's perception. And this second position perspective reminds us that we as industrialists are spenders of a limited bank account, not savers.

Everything in the system seems to have some sort of function. The more we study this, the more purposeful all elements appear to be. The stabilizing and evolutionary function of parasites in an ecosystem, for instance, is an ecological fact, though invisible. Again, the functions may be hard to comprehend before the system is influenced.

According to evolutionary theory, all life has the same origin. This means that all living forms are not only interconnected and mutually dependent on each other's existence. We can also say that all life is kindred. This is an interesting scientific parallel to the mystic or religious experiences of "being one with nature." Modern chaos theory shows how the principle of *self-similarity* is widespread in living forms and other systems. It should not be surprising, then, that self-similarity is a phenomenon crossing individuals and species. Evolutionary biology has focused near-sightedly on aggression, predation, and competition between (inter) and within (intra) species. In a larger perspective, however, it is evident that there is a hidden *interdependence* also between "enemies."[4]

How do the ecosystems manage, or: How are they managed? The answer simply is: "They do not or are not." This is now understood as *self-organizing*. As opposed to man-made technology, nature organizes production, consumption, and recirculation without external or internal management. In fact, Mother Nature seems to organize better without our "management," at least in the long run.

For this to work, it is essential not to break important feedback loops. We talk of two categories of feedback: negative and positive.[5] Negative feedback occurs when the information fed back to a subject leads to reestablishment of an equilibrium state. Thermostats are negative feedback mechanisms, both when they turn heat on and when they turn it off. Positive feedback is the opposite: Information fed back to the subject leads to more disequilibrium. Positive feedback then is deviation amplifying, where deviation refers to an initial equilibrium state. A company that dumps toxic waste in an irresponsible manner can be led to do that again through positive feedback: It's a great saving financially, and the company might do even more of it. Nondumping then is defined as an equilibrium state, financial saving as positive feedback leading to more dumping and more disequilibrium. Negative feedback could be represented by the dumping being brought to light, the market reacting, or the authorities imposing penalties. A bad conscience could also serve as negative feedback. These are all defined as negative, since they lead to a reestablishment of the defined equilibrium state of nondumping.

The classic example of positive feedback stems from Australia. A dozen European rabbits were introduced in 1859, and spread in the wild after the fence surrounding their region was destroyed. Within a half century, they became the worst pest ever to farmers. The positive feedback consists of course of "more rabbits making more rabbits," the initial number here being defined as the equilibrium state.

Positive and negative feedback loops can give contraintuitive results. The British authorities experienced an example of this when, at the end of the 1950s, they wanted to limit the population of wood pigeon. The method applied was mainly shooting, and more than two million pigeons were killed every year. The population, however, stayed stable. The key to understanding this situation is the knowledge that every year there is an excess of young pigeons. Shooting these birds leaves better feeding conditions and less intraspecific competition for the elder pigeons and their offspring. Hence, more successful breeding, and more pigeons![6] The authorities' common sense expectation was that mass shooting would start a positive feedback loop, at least for a time. Smaller numbers of pigeons ought to lead to smaller numbers of offspring. Instead, a negative feedback loop started, reestablishing equilibrium. How could anyone predict that the mass shooting of pigeons would lead to a stabilizing, in periods even an increase, of numbers? Often such feedback loops can only be "postdicted," not predicted.

A possible positive and threatening feedback loop might be activated if global warming is increased. Much solar warmth is now reflected back to space by the white polar ice. This reflection is a core factor in keeping the heat down. The ice layer, however, is rather thin. Small changes in the temperature of the earth can result in its melting away. This will lead to less reflection of heat, more global warming, more melting, and so on—a typical positive feedback loop.

Modern chaos theory operates with the concept of the butterfly effect, or SDIC—Sensitive Dependence on Initial Conditions. This means that future states of a system cannot possibly be predicted, since even small differences at the starting point of time can give enormous differences in the long run. Hence, a flitting butterfly in Bolivia may "cause" a storm in Malaysia. The natural ecosystems are regarded as unendingly complex, the numbers of feedback components forming chains and webs of a kind that cannot possibly be realistically simulated. This is a very important acknowledgment, the implication being that encompassing "eco-management" is a hopeless and dangerous mission.

As industrial man tends to think "as much as possible" this is not nature's way. Ecosystems tend to stabilize at optimum levels. The modern concept for this is "dynamic equilibrium." The concept signifies a level where different components are in balance, but that this is a living, changing point. Chaos theory indicates that dynamic equilibrium in fact gives a more rugged point of balance than static equilibrium. Warning signals should be sent out if the turn of the balance exceeds a certain critical minimum or maximum level. Population densities for differing populations and even species to survive have such critical minimum and maximum levels.

Ecosystems normally evolve very slowly. The web of feedback loops favors stability. Another factor securing stability is complexity. As the ecosystem gets older, it grows in complexity. New species develop, and old species diversify and specialize. More complex webs of feedback chains appear. Why this contributes to stability is a matter of common sense. If one species of green plants performed all of the photosynthesis, all life on earth would depend on this one plant species. A pest, or any factor threatening that species would threaten all life. A very unstable system! Instead, the system provides "back-ups" for most vital functions. The more species that can undertake vital functions, the more stable the system. Characteristic of stable ecosystems is *diversity*. The extreme counterexample is the man-made monocultures. Large fields of wheat or fish farms are examples.

Large wheat fields that are kept unvaried over many years can only be kept free from pests with the use of pesticides, and grow highly dependent on fertilizers. Fish farms depend on the use of antibiotic surplus. The lack of diversity is one explanation for their extreme vulnerability.

The concept of time is central in ecology. A key to understanding the perfection and stability of nature lies here. Over millions of years, a complex play of evolution and coevolution must have taken place. Fitness is ever improved, and a tremendous stability is reached. Turtles have remained mainly unchanged over 180 million years, the mussel for over 345 million years, and man for over 300,000 years.[7] Theoretically, an ecosystem can exist as long as the sun shines, and as long as it is left relatively undisturbed. In this perspective, modern industrial man is not even a child. If we check the relation between industrial man and nature from an imagined third position, industrial man's idea of managing and improving nature qualifies for a bed in a closed department of a mental hospital with the diagnosis of megalomania schizophrenia. To prevent any misunderstandings: This is not making a proposal. It is a corrective to our all-too-automatic first position perceptions. Let us summarize some of the characteristics of natural ecosystems.

Fundamental patterns of natural ecosystems:

—The ecosystems produce by the principle of local production for local consumption for local recirculation

—All elements have the same offspring—are kindred

—All elements are interrelated

—The ecosystems are self-organizing

—The ecosystems are mainly self-sufficient

—The ecosystems develop toward dynamic equilibrium through evolution

—The ecosystems are governed by complex feedback

—The ecosystems stabilize at optimum levels

—The ecosystems are dependent on a diversity of species and relations to maintain stability

—The ecosystems go through stages of development

—The ecosystem and its elements sometimes develop in nonlinear and unpredictable manners

—All elements in the ecosystems serve purposes or cover functions

—It is probable that ecosystems cannot be safely managed artificially

The understanding of these basic characteristics of ecosystems is important for two reasons. It gives a basis for a deeper understanding of the physiochemical eco-crisis and its possible solutions. It also provides a graceful metaphor which helps us to understand all life and all living systems better. At all times man has studied Mother Nature, both for enjoyment and for learning. The study of the ecosystems contains both qualities.

Chapter 4

Organizational Ecology

What is success? ... To leave the world a bit better whether by a
healthy child, a garden path, or a redeemed social condition.

Ralph Waldo Emerson

In this book the term "organizational ecology" refers to the points of
contact between ecology, environmentalism, organizations, and business.
These can be sorted into five main categories:

1. The ecosystem represents an aesthetic metaphor for all organized human systems, including business organizations.

2. Human ecologists, sociobiologists, and ethologists have shown us for a half
   century that industrial man carries his ancestors' genes, behavioral patterns, and
   emotions. In my opinion, organizational behavior simply cannot be understood
   adequately without these perspectives.

3. Humans are, throughout our evolutionary history, adapted to certain environmental conditions. When our modern environment deviates too radically from
   our natural niche, societies and individuals get ill.

4. Humans confront ecological crises all over the world. Organizational ecology
   provides a framework for understanding this, and the role of organized human
   activity in our attempt to cope with the crisis. Business plays a main role in this
   drama, and cannot escape the ethical challenges thrown out.

5. Environmentalism and greening of business open up a whole new world of
   business opportunities. Organizational ecology is also about how these opportunities should be seized.

THE ECOSYSTEM METAPHOR

The border separating natural science and social science is strong, and in my opinion, often rather unfruitful. It is based on the old dissention of nature versus nurture, inborn versus learned, genes versus culture. An either-or approach to this problem is unsatisfactory, not least because it often is based on a misunderstanding: the confusion of metaphor with reality. Let us shed light on this. For instance, the web of organizations in a community can be seen as an ecosystem. But this web of organizations *is not* literally an ecosystem.[1] The web of organizations and an ecosystem share essential characteristics. When we talk about evolutionary mechanisms in both systems, we should be very explicit as to whether we are referring to evolution in its scientific Darwinian meaning, or we are referring to a model, or a metaphor, which can be a source of useful understanding.

It should be noted that such metaphors are almost inevitable. Organizations are likened to football teams, organisms, families, armies, and data networks, to mention some examples.[2] Terms from these metaphors are applied all the time. When the sales manager asks his sales consultants to "play the ball," he does not mean it literally. When the CEO on kick-off talks about "our family tradition," he is not talking of family traditions at all. He is talking about the strong and lasting traditions of the company, to which he has a passionate relationship.

Trouble can arise when the distinction between literal meaning and metaphor is unclear. We find a bad example in Social Darwinism when it is misunderstood or misused: *Natural selection* is the mechanism that selects at random the genes best fitted to ensure survival under the prevailing environmental conditions at any time. It is a natural scientific concept. Bringing this into the social domain is obviously to use a metaphor. Genes are not units of interest in social systems science or in business life. But both between and inside companies, we too often hear expressions like "one of us had to win," or "that is nature's way, the strongest must survive." Natural selection is neither a scientific proof of social selection as a law of nature, nor should it provide an excuse for ruthless or egoistic action!By the way: The idea of evolution's preference of egoism as adverse to altruism is a theory, not a stated fact. The opposite view, that cooperation, altruism, and harmony are more typical than egoism, competition, and "selfish genes"[3] in natural systems, also has its proponents.[4] In fact, nature provides us with metaphors of both competition and cooperation, of egoism, and of altruism.

In the next part of this book we shall enter a totally *metaphorical* area of ecology. I shall apply the patterns of ecosystems to the individual business or organization. That an organization *is not* an ecosystem should be obvious by now. But both are systems. I regard the ecosystem as the "mother system" for systems of living organisms (and their environment). We can expect to find similarities between these categories of systems, and this may help us toward a new and clearer conception of the systems of organizations.

Organizational change meets with a whole array of different obstacles. It is no wonder, then, that attempts to find single success factors for good management and organizational optimizing do not succeed. Jokingly, it is claimed that the only success factor statistically proven to be a fact among managers is bodily height, tall managers being more successful than their smaller colleagues.

This lack of universal truth about success in management and organization is a strong argument for taking each initiative for organizational and managerial development at any point of time as an exceptional project, acknowledging that what works well in situation A could give bad results in situation B. It also is an argument for developing good theories that can be applied flexibly.

It seems to be a trend that management consultants are leaving the old paradigm of heavy analysis, followed by implementation and then a follow-up period. The new concept implies a continuity of analysis, implementation, and reevaluation repeatedly. I also share the opinion with many others that passive analysis is of less value than analysis through implementation. Only through implementation does the system at hand show its ability to change, its strengths, and its weaknesses.

In the next section an array of system patterns will be examined. We shall look to Mother Nature's ecosystem for inspiration to understand these patterns. But first, let us fit our concept of "hierarchy of system levels" into the picture. A top management group suffers badly from internal conflicts and negative communication. The CEO feels that something should be done, also because the conflicts seem to be spreading down the ranks. He discusses the situation with a management consultant. The consultant attends two meetings of the top management group, and then advises the CEO to start training the group in two areas. These include team building and goal-directed problem solving. The training is implemented and the group makes improvements. The improvements last for four months, after which there is a recession and the group is back to where it started. The conflicts take on speed in the lower ranks, however, both during and after the four months.

In this case, the management consultant gave advice based on the obvious: He saw bad team behavior and bad problem solving. Good team behavior and problem solving were needed, and his advice was intended to fill this need. Let us now ask, what did the consultant leave out in his evaluation of the situation? We can say that "conflicts and bad communication"/"team building and goal-directed problem solving" constitute level one in the hierarchy of system levels. The next level, setting the conditions for level one, would be the general condition of the whole enterprise, as illustrated in Figure 2.6. The next level up, society at large, then sets the conditions for the two lower levels. The company in the example above depended on a business niche that was in a decline. For general reasons, at this level three of the hierarchy the company soon could face bankruptcy. This set conditions for the lower levels, and leaving this out of the picture made the consultant conclude with wrong or insufficient interventions.

There are many examples of this. For instance, some years ago many banks in Norway showed bad financial results and had a bad reputation for service. A lot of training was initiated to teach the personnel service orientation and stress management, since this "obviously" was needed. But the results were disappointing, and the reason was clear: These actions had not touched on the basic conditions. Major restructuring and staff reductions were needed, and attempts to improve service before making these changes most often were in vain.

Business managers and business consultants share a common experience. When analyzing organizations, and when developing them, it seems easier to focus on the *less* important aspects. This is a parallel to the man searching for his lost keys in the light from a street lamp, which I mentioned in the introduction. We search where there is light, not in the dark, although the dark hides the keys. The well-intended actions directed at weak points often do not really hit the nail on the head. The less comprehensible areas of the organization are our concern in the following passages. They are hard to quantify, and it takes more wisdom than knowledge to handle them. But, at the same time, I believe them to be of a hierarchically overriding nature.

Part II

Organizations as Ecosystems

In their interrelationships, people move as in a dance, but they are unaware of their synchronized movement, and dance without music or choreography.

E. Hall, in Anthony Wilden, *The Rules Are No Game*
[author's translation]

Chapter 5

Common Interests and Conflict Solving

As to the first, you are to understand, that for above seventy moons past, there have been two struggling parties in this empire, under the names of Tramecksan, and Slamecksan, from the high and low heels on their shoes, by which they distinguish themselves. . . . The animosities between these two parties run so high, that they will neither eat nor drink, nor talk with each other.

Jonathan Swift, *Gulliver's Travels*

To develop a sound business, managers strive to establish common goals, common attitudes, a common culture. Edward Goldsmith, the pioneer of the periodical *The Ecologist*, labeled systems with common goals "homeotelic" systems. *Homeo* means common, and *telos* means goal, hence the term. The opposite is "heterotelic" systems. Homeotelic organizations are characterized by ruggedness and high productivity. Internal competition strengthens such systems and enhances their adaptive abilities. Heterotelic systems, on the other hand, are torn apart by internal competition and lose productivity.[1]

The existence of common goals seems to be an overriding criterion for success in business. A homeotelic system, however, should not be mistaken for an authoritarian system or a monoculture. The ideal of the homeotelic organization should be seen in connection with the ideals of 3rd order change-processes in organizations and the value of diversity, as will be elaborated on later. The *formal* existence of common goals in a company should not be confused with the *real* existence of such goals. Formality is one thing, reality something else.

ON THE BRINK OF A STRIKE

Let us first illustrate the problem of the homeotelic organization by describing a case: The example is a family company, with long traditions in the food-processing industry. Relations between management and workers have become increasingly strained over the past three years. The board of directors and the management have cooperated closely. Productivity is slowly declining, while the general trend in the trade is clearly positive. The board is dominated by members of the family.

The production workers make uncompromising wage demands and call for improvements in the working environment. On the verge of a strike, the management looks for a new CEO. An experienced man is found, who is given a wide range of authority. His mandate is to find a solution to the conflict and get the business back on a constructive path. Shortly afterward, he develops the following hypothesis of the situation.

The top management and production workers both suffer the misconception that their interests are basically conflicting ones. They seem to think one or the other of the parties has to win at the other's expense. They oppose each other in order to protect their own interests. It is this misconception that is at the core of the conflict. Here lies the possibility of a constructive solution, a solution involving the mutual acceptance of the common interest of both parties in the survival and further development of the business.

In order to change the situation, the following short-term measures are launched. The measures are accepted by the head of the family, who is also chairman of the board.

1. All family members, with the exception of the chairman, are to leave the board.

2. The management is to be given extensive authority in relation to the board.

3. All family members employed at different levels in the firm are to resign and find other employment.

4. The company is to be the main sponsor for the planned building of a community hall in the town.

5. In agreement with the unions, external consultants specializing in physical working environment are to be brought in. They are to evaluate the layout of all work places and give a written evaluation. This is to be reviewed jointly by the top management and the union leaders.

Within a month, the first four measures have been implemented and the fifth is underway. After a further six months, a substantial number of improvements in the physical working environment have been made. Productivity is rising (disregarding the costs incurred by the improvements to the working environment). The CEO feels that the time is right for a series of further measures to ensure a continued increase in productivity.

The development of a comprehensive strategy is started. The top management develops the company's vision with the board's support, and thereafter formulates the main goals for the coming two years. The vision and the main goals are discussed extensively with union representatives. Another goal is included on their initiative, directed toward improving the psychosocial working environment. In a comprehensive strategy process supported by the unions, representatives from all levels of the organization are involved in defining objectives and planning actions related to the main goals. Based upon this material, the CEO formulates a complete strategy document. The document is accepted by the management and the chairman of the board, and is finally presented at meetings to all levels of the company.

A management information system is established showing key figures for trends in productivity, turnover, profit, and market-related factors. Selected information from the management information system is now issued at regular intervals to the entire organization. Wage issues are included in fixed wage negotiations, and a great effort is made to establish objective criteria for wage increases. The main criteria agreed upon are: improvements in productivity and profitability, general wage increases in the industry, and evaluations of competitiveness based upon an analysis of the competition.

Within a year after implementation of these measures, the situation has changed dramatically. Productivity is steadily improving, and at a higher rate than for the competitors. Conflicts between management and unions are being resolved in a positive atmosphere through structured negotiations. Furthermore, the company has achieved a good reputation, following the completion of the community hall. Many factors contributed to the good results. The voluntary retreat from their positions on the part of some family members represented a strong signal of "peace" to the employees. All in all, however, the events can best be understood in the light of the following axiom.

Axiom I.1: Common Interests

Within the ecosystem, all components are kindred and interrelated. Individuals and groups within an ecosystem and within an organization are mutually dependent on each other and thereby have governing common interests. *Cooperation toward common goals should be the rule in organizations.*

The core of the problem was a deep conflict of interests between management and workers in a family company. The solution lay in the fact that the new CEO was able to look at the joint interests that were at stake from a mental third position. Both parties had been "blind" in the heated climate that had prevailed. They had only been able to see the situation from the first position. The main reason for the long-term program of improvements that was implemented in the organization was the admission of governing common interests. Overriding common goals were stressed, both in relation to keeping jobs and maintaining profitability. Furthermore, common interests were extended by the contribution to the town's community hall.

A general belief that there are governing common interests in all situations has far-reaching implications. The business community has long thought that the struggle between different groups, or levels, is natural and inevitable. In wage negotiations, for example, it is part of our language to talk about the "parties" involved. When we are able to look beyond these apparently conflicting interests, we find a number of solutions which otherwise are blocked. At the same time, we eliminate clichés such as "bad management versus good workers," or vice versa.

"Conflicts of interest" can be seen as misunderstandings resulting from poor communication. They also can be seen as differences of filters and punctuations. If either, or both, of the "parties" punctuate only their own short-term interests then "conflicts of interest" will occur. Ecologists and eco-philosophers have helped to promote the admission that "everything is interconnected."[2]

From the fourth position you either see that your filters are ones of common interests and win-win solutions, or ones of opposing interests. The idea of governing common interests in any situation should be seen as an ideal. To really see those, our ability to adopt all mental positions and to make different punctuations is put at stake. But governing common interests sometimes are hard to realize. Often it is easier to catch this perspective in retrospect. The common interests of the two superpowers, the United States and the USSR, during the cold war are now evident. The mutual suspicion in the context of the cold war made it impossible for the parties to see the common interests of peaceful coexistence and social and scientific cooperation.

An open hand may be understood as an expression of a will for peace or as a tactical maneuver, depending on the context. In hot situations, the ability to see common interests too often disappears. At a distance it is easy to see the common interests and the potential win-win solutions, be this for Israel and Palestine, Serbs and Croats, black South Africans and Boers. But under stress, mutual suspicion grows in society, as it does in organizations. The establishment of common goals, open communication, tolerance to differences of opinion, and honesty make the best climate for homeotelism.

Negotiations take place in all organizations: on internal decisions, formal negotiations, and with representatives of the environment. In the following section I shall describe a prototype model for win-win negotiations. According to our sorting of change-processes in three categories, this should represent a 3rd order negotiation process.

3RD ORDER NEGOTIATION PROCESS

It is a frequent misconception that in order to find a common conclusion, one must first agree on the facts of the present situation, and also preferably on the past. But there are just as many facts as there are people involved. If we look at the purpose of negotiation, namely, to find solutions, it is clear that the emphasis should be placed on the future and change, rather than on the past. Good negotiations should result in a win-win situation. The focus should be on how to best look after the particular interest of all parties.

A negotiation situation may consist of an everyday communication situation, a sales situation, the resolution of a minor conflict, or a formal situation around the conference table. In order to make all points as clear as possible, let us now consider a formal negotiation situation.

As an introduction, it is often advisable to establish *agreement on the purpose* of the negotiation (namely, to find a satisfactory/positive/constructive/useful solution to the situation). If attention is constantly focused on the problem, it can be useful to redefine it as a "common challenge" or similar. Furthermore, it can be useful to achieve *agreement on the importance* of the negotiation. The idea is to motivate participants to really find a solution, and make it difficult for the parties to "opt out" when the negotiations enter a more difficult stage. *Agreement on trying to agree* also acts as a commitment and fulfills these three preliminary "agreements." Together, this gives an atmosphere where common interests are central. If temperatures are high, is it important to achieve agreement on frames and negotiating rules, right down to the smallest detail; who is to guide the process and how it is to proceed.

Let us now illustrate the 3rd order negotiation model. I call the parties A and B.

Model for 3rd order negotiation:

1. Goal.

a. Agreement on the purpose of the negotiations. This is formulated at a high enough logical level (general formulation) to make it easy to achieve agreement. (Thereafter follows possible agreement on importance, agreement on agreeing, and agreement on guidelines, as mentioned above).

b. Summary of interests. Agreement on common interests is established first, followed by mutual agreement on the respective parties' particular interests. Agreement is then established on how to find solutions which, as far as possible, cover all these interests. The interests are formulated at as low a logical level as possible, but still being accepted by the other party.

    c. Summary of what has been agreed upon. A check is made on the parties to ensure that a solution covering the formulated and accepted interests is a solution that will be accepted by them.

2. Summary of facts. Here the parties agree about what has happened and is happening, and what the consequence of the existing state of affairs and solutions (or lack of them) will be. (Prolonged effort to reach agreement at a low logical level is unnecessary and tends to create conflict. With few exceptions, the achievement of quick agreement at a less precise level is to be preferred.)

3. Brainstorming. Generating alternative solutions that cover common interests, party A's interests and party B's interests respectively.

4. Sorting and evaluation. Here we summarize all proposals and the least valid are discarded. The proposals are then collated to form a preconclusion, or a possible solution. This preconclusion should not be binding.

5. Preconclusion appraisal. The preconclusion is made the subject of a critical impact analysis. It is evaluated from the parties' first, second, and third position. During the appraisal, the preconclusion is refined. A whole or partial return to brainstorming can be undertaken periodically, if necessary.

6. Agreement. The agreement should be specified in detail to avoid any misunderstandings.

One party's special interests are often unacceptable to the other party. This is a key issue in negotiation. An unacceptable special interest is made acceptable by means of the hierarchy of means and ends, that is, by moving up from the unacceptable mean to its acceptable end. By this, *all special interests can be made acceptable to the other party*. If the initial formulation of the end is not sufficient, the special interests can be formulated at the next highest level. Let us shed light on this with an example: During legal proceedings where a man and a woman were to part company after twelve years of marriage, both claimed custody of their ten-year-old, only child. This was the most important special interest for both parties. The family counsellor made the parties see that custody of the child was a means. He then asked for their respective ends. The man's special interest formulated as an end was: a guarantee that he would not be pushed to one side in the future, but would in fact still be the child's father. The woman's special interest formulated as an end was: assurance that the child would receive necessary daily care in such practical matters as having clean clothes and a correct diet. Formulated in this manner, both parties could fully accept the other's special interests (Figure 5.1). This proved to be the turning point in the proceedings. A cooperation contract was drawn up which adequately covered these special interests.

The parties' common interests are acceptable for both parties by definition. Common interests usually comprise things like retaining a good

Figure 5.1
How to Move from Means to Ends in Conflict Solving. The conflicting parties'
respective interests are made acceptable to the other party by moving upwards
from means to ends. The potential for a win-win solution lies in the boxes
containing question marks.

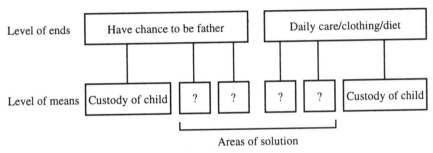

spirit of cooperation, to keep up a good reputation, and so on. Furthermore, they concern the synergetic effect generated by cooperation as compared to opposition.

Completion of item 1 is important. In order to finalize this phase, all
necessary interests must be brought out into the open. Unless this is done
thoroughly, the parties will return to this stage ad infinitum. The item
could be finalized in the following manner: "So, if we arrive at a solution
together where X, Y, and Z are taken care of . . . is this acceptable to party
A and party B?" We can avoid a premature completion of this item by
questions such as: "What more/is there anything more which should be
taken care of?" or "I have a feeling there is something we have forgotten. . . ."

It is useful to have an interval between items 2 and 3. Brainstorming
needs to be done in as relaxed an atmosphere as possible. Item 3, for
instance, can begin with "How do we achieve the goal(s) we have set
ourselves? Let's think freely about this for a few moments without any
preconceptions. How can we look after all the interests that are at stake?"
As in all brainstorming, only creative thinking is relevant. Evaluation and
criticism are irrelevant here and should be ended immediately.

Impartial criteria should be emphasized during item 4. It should also be
respected that the individual party is a specialist in knowing whether a
proposal will take care of his/her interests. A brief return to item 3 can
be useful if a proposal is thought to contain even more possibilities than
those formulated so far.

The 3rd order negotiation process can extend over a period of one hour
or up to several years. The process operates best if led by a neutral third
party. Otherwise, during heated discussions, it is difficult to keep track of
the process or keep the phases and frames clear of obstructions. The process assumes a minimum of willingness to negotiate, and a minimum of

mutual confidence in the other party's keeping to any agreement at all. Most often, a lot of activities to lower emotional tension are needed before the process described is at all applicable. In some situations, win-win solutions are blocked. If one or both parties are untrustworthy, unwilling to negotiate, or simply only take first position, 3rd order negotiations cannot take place.

CHECK YOUR COMPANY: COMMON INTERESTS

You can easily check the degree of consensus in your management group:

- Let each manager independently fill in the matrix of internal strengths and weaknesses (see Figure A3.1) in your business. To which degree do the answers overlap?
- Let each manager independently rank possible strategic goals or objectives. To which degree do the lists correlate?

Other questions:

- Are win-win solutions and attitudes the more common in the company?
- How often do managers engage themselves in problem solving horizontally in your organization?
- How well informed of problems and challenges in other departments or divisions are your managers?
- How well do the union representatives and the management in your business solve problems together?

CHECK YOURSELF: COMMON INTERESTS

- Do you feel personally that all levels and divisions basically have common interests?
- Do you use the common strategy as point of reference when you make decisions?
- Apply the questions above to yourself.

Chapter 6

Self-Organizing

The wisdom you gave me, entwines me in mysteries, and the candles
you lit, lead only to darkness.

Bjoernstjerne Bjoernson, *Collected Works*, vol. 10
[author's translation]

Natural ecosystems adapt to changing environments, as do organizations. All living systems seem to contain the ability for *self-organizing*. By this we mean that any group, be it at a starting point ever so chaotic, will exhibit organizing activities. Hierarchies, division of work, systems of information, or communication will emerge. Order will come out of chaos.

The principle of self-organizing supplements our understanding of the value of the 3rd order change-process. Self-directive teams, self-organizing fractals, delegation of tasks to lower levels, activation of the lower ranks in problem solving; why is it so important? Self-organizing supplements our answer. We might say that self-organizing represents an ideal: If the system at hand has the necessary resources and competence, it should be given the opportunity to self-organize. (A further discussion on the preconditions for 3rd order processes, and thereby for self-organizing, is given in Chapter 18.)

The question of self-organizing may be best illustrated in situations where international aid meets with local resistance, a phenomenon well-known to the staff of international aid organizations. The concept of self-organizing provides us with a new tool to understand such resistance. The self-organizing nature of communities is provoked in situations of aid-giving. Social stability depends on the slow coevolution of technology, social institutions, culture, and economy. These are elements of the self-organizing processes in action at community level. External help into the system runs the risk of disturbing these sensitive and complex mechanisms. Let us illustrate the point in another context: An organ implanted into a living organism is naturally expelled. It represents a violation of the body's self-organizing principles.

The principle applies equally well to the arena of individual change. Most therapists have learned that the idea of taking over and deciding for a client represents a losing strategy. Even the best of advice often is not received or utilized. We understand this counterintuitive situation better when we see that even an individual is an example of a self-organizing system. This also helps us to understand the power of metaphoric communication. Many influential, wise men talk in metaphors, as did Jesus Christ. Metaphoric communication leaves room for self-organizing on the part of the receiver, and resistance is diminished.

Capable management consultants have an intuitive understanding of this principle. They follow the ideal of working through the people in the organization, keeping themselves as invisible as possible. They also do their best to hand over their own competence to the client, giving him the opportunity to exercise self-organizing and achieve future self-sufficiency. The desired result is stability and adaptability on the part of the client.

Axiom I.2: Self-Organizing

Ecosystems and organizations cannot be managed from the outside without high risk of erroneous prediction and instability of the system.
Self-organizing should be the aim in organizations.

Social systems can be hard to understand from the outside. For one thing, industrial man has failed to understand the wisdom of "superstition" in the third and fourth worlds. The people in India, for example, have institutions of *Khamadenu*, holy trees, and *Kalpaturu*, holy cows. But these ideas are very functional. Modern forestry ruins their ecosystem, the rural people included. Moreover, eating the cows means eradicating the main source of manure, fuel, work, and food. Even the idea of giving the holy soil a share of the yield is ecologically wise, not "irrational." Only self-organizing can take care of stability in these complicated systems.

The ecological megatrend will favor self-organizing on all scales: for societies, communities, and organizations. In an article on the future factory, Peter F. Drucker introduces the concept of the "flotilla" company: "The plant of 1999 will be a 'flotilla,' consisting of modules centered either around a stage in the production process or around a number of closely related operations. Though overall command will still exist, each module will have its own command and control."[1] This agrees well with our concept of self-organizing, as well as with the principle of local production for local consumption for local recirculation, and thereby paints a desirable picture of the future from an ecological point of view.

We find a new metaphor of the rules of self-organizing in fractal geometry. It is well-known that similarity over scales, that is, *self-similarity* is a natural phenomenon. At the Fraunhofer-Institute in Stuttgart, Germany, this is taken as a sound metaphor for organizing principles. The companies that they reorganize are built up from "fractals," that is, smaller units that share self-similarity with the whole, and with self-similar goal structures from top to bottom.[2] Each fractal is made up of self-organizing teams, and the idea of rotating leadership is applied. As far as this is suitable for the purpose, the fractals also are developed into independent and self-organizing SBUs (Strategic Business Units).

A NOTE ON SELF-SUFFICIENCY

For third and fourth world countries, a growing dependency on trade with the first world threatens their chance to self-organize and thereby stabilize.[3] The green revolution contained one sound element: It aimed at developing the countries of the third and fourth world in the direction of self-sufficiency. The enhanced production was intended for the local market, to defeat hunger and poverty. It failed many places, but the intention was sound.

The new revolution now leading the edge of international help to developing countries heads for development of these countries through participation on the world market. The first world shall deliver new biotechnology, in the form of capital, know-how, equipment, and goods, and the third world shall produce for sale on the international market. It is easy to predict that this strategy will lead to new failures and more poverty. The basic reason is that it represents a new and long step away from self-sufficiency for each country as a whole, and for local communities. It implies an increase in dependency and a parallel increase in the potential social instability.

Even the United States, seen as a heavy actor in the global market, has an economy based mainly on self-sufficiency. Exports constitute only 10.6% of GNP, and imports are 11.1%, and these numbers remain more or less stable over time. This implies, as the economist Paul Krugman shows, a relative independence of national living standards from international competitiveness.[4] To recommend or support a development in countries that are weak competitors, in the direction of greater dependency on unstable and uncontrollable external factors, has to be unwise.

CHECK YOUR COMPANY: SELF-ORGANIZING

- Are SBUs, groups, and individuals, as far as realistically possible, given opportunity to self-organize?
- Do authority, responsibility, and accountability overlap in your business?
- Do your managers follow progressive plans for further delegation of authority to lower levels?

CHECK YOURSELF: SELF-ORGANIZING

- How often do you disregard a decision on a lower level contrary to the opinion of the person responsible?
- And how often do you realize afterward that the person responsible would have reached a right decision if you had given him the time and chance?
- Do you have a plan for further delegation of authority to lower levels over time?
- Do you practice minimum or maximum control of lower levels?

Chapter 7

Optimums, Not Maximums or Minimums

Rather, for all objects and experiences, there is a quantity that has optimum value. Above that quantity, the variable becomes toxic. To fall below that value is to be deprived.

Gregory Bateson, *Mind and Nature*

PRODUCTIVITY

Productivity is a description of what we get out of our resources relative to the resources spent. Productivity is the relationship between output and input. This applies to every field of activity and to every type of value-creating enterprise. We can formulate this as a general formula:

$$\text{Productivity} = \frac{\text{Any expression for created value/Output}}{\text{Any expression for contributory factors/Input}}$$

Thinking along the lines of simple cause-and-effect in business, this would appear to be quite straightforward: It's simply a matter of minimizing use of resources and maximizing the amount of value created. Put briefly, a maximum productivity level should be the aim in every situation. But it's not quite as simple as that. Quantity is not always the same as quality, be it a question of sugar in your coffee, drugs to treat illness, or profit in business. The following incident should illustrate this point.

The Italian branch of a German corporation manufacturing electric tools has been given a budget for the year where the profit is stipulated at $1.2 million. However, changes in the marketplace make it possible to take a larger profit margin on certain key products than was first calculated, and also to increase market share in a certain segment of the market. The Italian management reports back to the corporate management, presenting the positive prognoses together with plans on how to achieve a profit increase of 60%. To their surprise, the reaction from corporate management is unequivocally negative. The Italians are refused permission to change their profit target and are told to limit their market share to a given level. The corporate management had established optimum long-term goals, and knew that deviations over or under a set limit would affect these. To the Italian, "as much as possible" managers, the refusal from the corporate management to accept the plans was incomprehensible.

In a healthy organization, productivity will stabilize around an *optimum* productivity level. To define this level is no easy task. I believe the following criteria to be theoretically valid.

Criteria for optimum productivity:

1. Productivity is sufficiently high for the company to operate with a long-term profit.

2. Productivity is sufficiently high for the company to be competitive.

3. Effectiveness and work tempo do not impair health, neither physical nor mental health.

4. Productivity is low enough to avoid unnecessary "forcing" of competition in the industry in general.

Let us illustrate the struggle to find an optimum level with an example: The company is a sales organization. It has a sales department comprising eighty salesmen, four sales managers and sales directors, as well as a sales administrator. The company sells four different products on West European markets.

The previous year and the last six months had been bad periods for the company. Sales had steadily decreased. The board and the management required a certain level of turnover, profitability, and productivity. The sales department was unable to live up to these expectations. In order to stimulate increased sales, the sales staff were rewarded individually with extra payment and other material benefits. Commands and detailed work instructions became the order of the day. The organization had become unbalanced, as illustrated by the need for more and more rewards, stricter orders, and even more detailed instructions. At one point the salesmen expected extra bonus points for turning up for work in the morning!

Two professional board members were asked to involve themselves directly in the working of the sales department, in order to carry out training and to analyze the situation. Thereafter, optimum productivity levels were defined by mutual discussion. It turned out that these levels were defined at a very much *lower* level than the original level which the board and the management had required. The board and the management recognized the need to break this vicious circle. For the most part, the optimum productivity levels were accepted, and certain conditions were made to ensure that they could be raised at a later stage. This comprised training and the systematic definition of secondary tasks, together with minor reorganization.

A five-week plan was established, with a gradual increase in turnover, profitability, and productivity up to the required level as formulated in the strategy. Methods of improvement were continually identified, evaluated, and implemented by the sales supervisors in cooperation with the salesmen, sales directors, and the two board members. By means of this process, control over the situation was fully restored. The attitude of the salesmen changed. They became motivated by salesmanship as a profession and by wanting to do a good job for the company. The management delegated a large degree of responsibility and authority to the sales supervisors, who in turn delegated to the salesmen. In addition, the employees were involved in working out and implementing plans and information systems.

The pressure on making productivity grow is strong in an environment of international competition. One of the effects of the principle of local production for local consumption for local recirculation will be to ease this pressure. This will leave more space for choice and self-organizing of tempos and production methods for local communities.

TOO MANY CHANGES OVER TOO SHORT A PERIOD

A high-tech research company had been through a two-year program of organizational development. During this time, work had been devoted to strategy development, strategy implementation, and productivity improvement. An extensive management-information system had been introduced, and a comprehensive program aimed at improving management competence had been completed.

The results of the program were excellent, and forces within the company were eager to continue the process. They succeeded in getting their proposal accepted. This was to establish a new program which would include a complete personnel plan for the company. Key persons in the organization welcomed the new program, and large-scale planning was started. To the surprise of the external consultants and management, work came to a complete halt after a few weeks. Deadlines and agreements were repeatedly delayed. The reports and studies which were eventually produced were of very poor quality. The potential for a conflict in the organization grew substantially.

At a meeting with the managing director and personnel director, the new external consultants reviewed the company history and were informed in detail about the programs that had been conducted during the past five years. They arrived, jointly, at the following hypothesis.

The organization was currently saturated with change. All "resistance" to further processes should be understood as being an expression of the need for stabilization at the current level. After some debate, the top management decided that the new program should be stopped. An exception was made for some preparatory work, to be done over a period of time. The program was to be restarted in another two years or so, but then on a slightly smaller scale. The potential for a conflict in the organization was immediately reduced. The positive level of productivity that had been achieved before the disruption was reestablished, and the climate developed positively.

Axiom I.3: Theoretical Optimums

For all ecosystems and organizations there is a theoretical optimum level of productivity, and an optimum balance between stabilizing activity and adaptive change.
Formulation of optimum, not maximum or minimum, goals and actions should be the rule in organizations.

This high-tech research company experienced to the full that "more" is not necessarily "better." There is an optimum point of balance between stability and change. It is as if the system refuses to implement further action when the amount of changes reaches a certain level. We can interpret this as the system's inherent tendency to maintain a level of stability. Resistance to change is not ill will or reactionary thinking. The opposite is rather the case. Resistance is a healthy expression of the system's ability to take care of identity and integrity, and thereby stability.

CHECK YOUR COMPANY: OPTIMUMS

You can easily check whether optimum standards are established in the company:

• Make and distribute a questionnaire among managers and a sample of co-workers where they are asked to give a quantified description of the standard of volume and/or quality in different areas. Compare the answers with each other, and with an optimum standard for the matter at hand.

Other questions:

• Do managers and co-workers have clear pictures of both what is too much and what is too little in their most important areas of activity?

- Are goals and objectives honestly quantified, so that deviations are unwanted, be they above or below the set level?
- Is there a general agreement on norms for productivity in the company?

CHECK YOURSELF: OPTIMUMS

- Apply the questions above to yourself.
- Do you sometimes celebrate that you have fulfilled a task or reached an objective?
- Are you able to leave a task even when you see possible improvements?
- Can you say "no" to taking on tasks or to accepting offers?
- Do you have a clear picture of what your optimum performance and an optimum career would look like?

Chapter 8

Feedback and Openness

"I only scream to have a good conscience," explained the Mymble's daughter and looked very important. "When mummy left she said: "I'm leaving your little sister to you and if you can't bring her up, then nobody can, because I gave up right from the start." "Well, now I understand," said Moomin-daddy. "Carry on screaming if it calms you down."
Tove Jansson, *The Exploits of Moominpappa* [author's translation]

Without feedback we cannot function. Our senses provide feedback on our surroundings and on how our surroundings react toward us. Interpersonally, we constantly give each other feedback. Sometimes this is nonverbal, at other times we use words. Feedback is a precondition for cooperation and learning.

An open system both receives and transmits feedback. It is adaptable and flexible. This applies to all levels within systems: individuals, departments, and organizations. To exchange feedback is something that really ought to go without saying—like eating and drinking—and it should be done when things go right as well as when they go wrong. Says Peter Drucker: "Quality circles ... have been successful in Japan because they came in after SQC (Statistical Quality Control) had been established. As a result, both the quality circle and management have objective information about the effects of workers' suggestions. In contrast, most U.S. quality circles of the last 20 years have failed despite great enthusiasm, especially on the part of workers. The reason? They were established without SQC, that is, without rigorous and reliable feedback."[1]

IMPLEMENTING CHANGE BY MEANS OF FEEDBACK

I shall illustrate the question of feedback in organizations with an example. This is about a sales organization in the data and office equipment business. This company had been trying to adapt itself to reach new market segments for two years. Specifically, the company wanted to become a general supplier for as many big customers as possible. In their day-to-day work, however, the salesmen continued to sell where they found it easiest. This applied particularly to small-scale sales to small customers whom they knew well. The management was determined to develop the business in the new direction, but had to admit that they had failed to succeed in practice. A thorough review of the situation together with external consultants resulted in the following hypothesis.

The directives from the management had barely been understood by the sales teams, and certainly not taken seriously. This was because they were not being followed through. The directives were perceived as being pro forma instructions. The salesmen considered it justifiable to follow or not to follow the directives as it suited them. There were no systems of two-way feedback in this regard, and no practice of such. Additionally, it was evident that the salary system, which rewarded sales by volume regardless of market segment, encouraged the salesmen to go for quick and easy sales, irrespective of market segment.

Based on this understanding, a series of measures was implemented. First, all the sales teams were brought together, and the reason for the desired change in customer segmentation was explained. Clear and detailed written information also was given, emphasizing the importance of reaching the new market segments for maintaining long-term profitability. Second, a sales-related management information system was developed in cooperation with the salesmen. This system showed sales trends in relation to the market segments on a weekly basis.

A system was developed to link salary to results in the different market segments. This was accepted by the salesmen. Half-yearly appraisal meetings were also introduced in the company. These included a sequence of mutual feedback between superior and subordinate. Seminars under the heading "feedback" were arranged for sales managers.

After eight months the proportion of sales to the new market segments increased from 36% to 52% of total sales. There were no organizational problems connected with this situation. What happened? Our next axiom may be of interest.

Axiom I.4: Feedback

To adapt successfully, ecosystems and organizations are dependent on feedback. Systems that are too closed to feedback degenerate and/or die out, systems that are too open are vulnerable and lose identity.

Free flow of relevant feedback should be the rule inside organizations, and they should be characterized by an optimum degree of openness to the environment.

The management wanted to have systematic control over certain market segments. The hypothesis that was drawn up can be summarized in the concept of feedback: Undesirable behavior did not have any consequences, either economically or as social feedback.

An organization without feedback lacks effective control. Good intentions are not enough in relation to constructive development and change. In this example, training was given in giving feedback, and a sales-related management information system was installed at the same time. This system gave weekly feedback directly related to the changes that the management wanted to implement.

Organizations that have problems, or are unable to adjust to change, are often characterized by the lack of, and shortcomings in, feedback. In some cases, organizational cultures are formed where people protect each other from feedback: "I won't criticize you if you don't criticize me." "The learning organization" is a popular slogan. The key prerequisite is feedback.

FEEDBACK PROCESSES

If I ever had an opportunity to teach all managers one single, interhuman competence, my choice would fall on feedback. This covers the ability to both receive and give feedback. The following is a basic lesson.

The giving of feedback should have an aim, and not only the one of "getting it off one's chest."

When difficult feedback has to be given, it is best done face-to-face. Feedback given orally has qualities not found in written feedback. This is fairly obvious, considering the fact that most of the information communicated consists of nonverbal signals. When interhuman feedback is given by letter or EP (Electronic Post), this nonverbal information is left out. In a face-to-face situation, misunderstandings can be cleared up, and a mutual process of learning can take place between the participants.

Feedback may quite simply be a matter of telling others what they are doing wrong, and how things should be done. We could call this a 1st order feedback process. It can also take the form of a presentation of a given set of alternatives, and asking the other person to choose from these himself. This would be a 2nd order feedback process. The following is a model designed to activate the recipient of the feedback into generating alternatives him/herself, in accordance with common goals; that is, a 3rd order feedback process.

Model for 3rd order feedback process:

1. Goal.

   a. Purpose of the feedback. The purpose of the feedback should be clearly stated and should be agreed upon. This would normally imply achieving an improvement in the standard of work as well as providing learning.

   b. Purpose of the action covered by the feedback. The purpose or aim of the action(s) covered by the feedback should be agreed upon.

2. Discussion of the action(s). Here we try to obtain some agreement on what actually happened, especially what the recipient of the feedback chose to do or omitted to do, and of the implications. (Precise agreement on "what really happened" is seldom necessary when the main purpose is improvement and learning.)

3. Brainstorming. This is a creative phase aimed at finding alternative methods of behavior. Deadlock in a dilemma between two lines of approach (one presented by the person giving feedback and one by the recipient) should be avoided. The purpose of brainstorming is to create an atmosphere of free and independent thinking, and to generate more than one or two alternatives.

4. Sorting and evaluation. A summary of the alternatives thrown up during the brainstorming session, as well as their evaluation with regard to the purpose/aim clarified under item 1.b. Preconclusion of the best alternative(s).

5. Preconclusion appraisal. Impact analysis of the preconclusion from first, second, and third positions.

6. Decision. Agreement on a specific conclusion, preferably with a given trial period and with agreement on follow-up.

As we can see, the model for 3rd order feedback has the same structure as for 3rd order negotiation. This is not really surprising, since feedback may in fact be seen as an example of a negotiation process, where persons A and B negotiate an agreement for the future. Good feedback is learning-oriented, change-oriented, and future-oriented. It differentiates clearly between case and person.

The lack of feedback in organizations may be the explanation not only of low learning abilities, but also low motivation. Reward belongs to the category of feedback. Let us look at reward in organizations for a moment, especially the preconditions for its efficiency. One of these is closeness in time between action and reward. Closeness in time also ensures that the link between performance and reinforcement is perceived. If the reward for a good performance is delayed until after a period of bad performance, it may unconsciously be perceived as a reward for bad performance, or that it really does not matter how you perform. Feedback in the form of rewards also should be perceived as just. The checking of this beforehand is essential. Feedback can be perceived as neutral information, as punishment, or as praise. Praising cultures develop less anxiety and more stability. Cultures dominated by punishment tend to develop antagonistic subcultures and clashes of interest.

A last case to be mentioned is the case of "feedback to the wrong recipient." In insecure cultures this is common; people generally dare not give the proper feedback to the responsible person. Instead they give it to someone whom they feel confident in, just to get things off their chest. The results of such feedback can enter into a positive feedback loop resulting in organizational paranoia.

NOT TOO OPEN, NOT TOO CLOSED

An ecosystem is generally a closed system. A company, on the other hand, is largely an open system. In the last chapter, I spoke about optimum levels of productivity, market shares, and economic results. In the same way, here we can imagine an optimum level for openness for a company in relation to its environment.

The discipline of family therapy is rich in concepts describing different systems. The idea of optimum openness is very relevant here. A too-closed family system, a socially isolated family, easily develops psychiatric patterns. Typical symptoms are various categories of psychosis. Overinvolvement between family members creates an atmosphere of oversensitivity and dependence. The family world is everything, and should fulfill all needs, which it of course cannot do. At the other extreme, the too-open family system lets in everybody. The psychiatric pattern here tends more toward criminality and antisocial attitudes, including drug addiction. It is interesting to see these patterns, of course, in a less psychiatric version, when organizations are too open or too closed in relation to their environment. Let us look at a case of "too open," from the world of business and industry.

A chain of computer equipment dealers started to notice a drop in turnover when price competition tightened. The business was typical of the trade: young, dynamic, and market-oriented. The information systems used to monitor market fluctuations and product development were extremely good. During the first years of trading, they had profiled themselves in the following order of priority: as being the cheapest, having the greatest choice, and as being specialists in the supply of various assorted parts. At an emergency board meeting in the organization, the following hypothesis for the shortfall in turnover was reached.

The stagnation in sales was attributed to the fact that customers felt no sense of loyalty toward the company. This was because the company changed its profile too often. If a market survey indicated that price was a determining factor for a particular target group, then price was profiled. If customers showed a preference for dealing with large suppliers, this feature was profiled. The customers could easily justify shifting suppliers because the company had no stable identity. The following measures were taken.

A conference was arranged, attended by members of the board, the company management, and external consultants. The objective was to develop a company profile which included determining inherent values. The identity that was currently lacking was to be established. As a result of the conference, the business description, values, and vision were determined. All the elements included were marketed extensively throughout the organization. This was achieved through both written information and meetings attended by all employees. All advertising and information material issued by the company afterward was profiled in the same manner.

These changes were followed by another difficult year, after which turnover slowly increased. The share of sales consisting of new sales to existing customers rose. The number of new customers recommended to the company by one or more existing customers also rose. The company was able to maintain a slow and stable growth in a market where a number of its competitors faced bankruptcy.

This company could be described as being typically market-driven. It was an example of a too-open system and, as cited in the above axiom: vulnerable, and with a lost identity. Actions to develop and implement such an identity were the key to achieving positive change.

On the other hand, there are frequent examples that correspond to what the axiom calls "closed systems." These are businesses that do not gather or respond to market impulses and which live in their own closed world. Quality control from outside agents is a means to open up the system. Another is surveys of customer satisfaction. A third is benchmarking among competitors. Closed organizations are neither flexible nor open to change. They lack the vitality that external impulses can give. Such organizations will in time degenerate or be outclassed by others.

CHECK YOUR COMPANY: FEEDBACK

You can easily check whether feedback is working in your company:

- Ask managers to rate their professional and interhuman competencies seen from their subordinates' point of view. Ask the subordinates to rate their managers by the same criteria. Check to which degree the answers overlap.
- Ask co-workers at all levels to list and quantify strategic and operational objectives. Ask them (a) to indicate whether their own activity influences their fulfillment or not, and (b) the status regarding the different objectives. Check with authorized information. Other questions:
- Do you frequently check your market's and your customers' perception of your company?
- Is there a clear connection between performance and rewards in the company?

- Is fair and frank feedback upward in the organization rewarded or punished?
- When employees are promoted, are the selections generally understood and accepted or do they cause surprise and discussions? (If feedback is practiced, selections do not cause surprise and discussion.)
- Are reports on results systematically fed back to those who created the results?
- Are appraisal meetings regularly arranged between managers and subordinates?

CHECK YOURSELF: FEEDBACK

- How well do you separate your personal likes and dislikes of co-workers from your perception of their real performance?
- Do you give frank and direct feedback upward, downward, and horizontally in the organization, whenever you find it relevant?
- Can you stay calm and focus on outcomes when other people criticize you?
- When you give feedback, are you conscious of your choice of time and place?
- How good are you at focusing on outcomes and learning when you give feedback?
- Do you actively elicit feedback from others?
- Are you a good listener?
- Are you able to model the behavior of other people when appropriate?
- Are you able to not model the behavior of people with authority when appropriate?
- Are you able to say "no?"

Chapter 9

The Role of Diversity

Ontological, cultural and genetic diversities are prime movers of life's richness.

Henryk Skolimowski, *Living Philosophy*

The principle of diversity balances the principle of the homeotelic organization. The principle of homeotelism shows the importance of sharing basic goals. But sharing basic goals should not mean sharing all opinions or values. In ecosystems the role of diversity is evident. Even parasites seem to be necessary and to have a stabilizing function. Simulations of ecosystems indicate this. Simulated ecosystems with parasites give rise to more species by evolution. This may be understood as the parasites forcing their hosts to develop; they enter into an evolutionary arms race. This again leads to differences in species, and growing diversity. As we have seen, the stability of the ecosystem depends on diversity of species.

Our times have too many examples of artificially established biological monocultures. Be it wheatfields or fish farms, the picture is the same. These cultures are highly unstable, and are vulnerable to pests. The tons of antibiotics needed to keep pests away tell the story all too well. Let us formulate this as an axiom.

Axiom I.5: Diversity

Diversity is conditional for evolution, adaptation, and stability in ecosystems and in organizations. Monocultures are naturally destroyed and/or die out. *Diversity should characterize organizations.*

The metaphor of diversity is a strong reminder to the authoritarian manager who wants everybody to be like himself. A more constructive attitude is to welcome differences in style, culture, and opinion. It is a bad sign when everyone is in complete agreement, or when managers start to select for hire or promotion only those who are like them.

The principle should also question some organizational "truths." For example, is it desirable that all hands are similar: top-efficient, competent, outcome-oriented, and sensible? Or is it, quite the opposite, important that there are some "parasites," some dissenters? Is it even of importance to have some conflicts? It is tempting to answer a "yes" to these questions. The value of differences is quite universal. To have a representation of "good," we must also have "bad." To have a sense of sound competition, or evolutionary pressure in the organization, there must be differences. If we draw them, the conclusions are very counterintuitive. There could be situations where you consciously choose to hire the second or third "best," giving priority to differences and sound tension in a group!

Degeneration can sometimes be observed in organizations where everything is uniform. Examples of such monocultures are similar age groups, sexes, and cultural backgrounds. Variety is a criterion for positive "tension," and, at the same time, for long-term stability. There must be a certain degree of internal variety in order to ensure adequate tension and vitality.

Authoritarian regimes of different colors have demonstrated very well the results of social monocultures. It seems to be a good idea to learn from their bad experiences and to avoid this state of affairs.

The sound enterprise promotes differences and disagreements!

CHECK YOUR COMPANY: DIVERSITY

- Are different points of view represented in the management?
- Are managers and other employees of different sex, age, and cultural origin?
- Are lively discussions generally encouraged?

CHECK YOURSELF: DIVERSITY

- Do you tend to hire people who are as similar as possible to yourself?
- Do you actively seek people whom you know will present opposing views to your own?
- How is diversity represented among your friends and family?

Chapter 10

Conditions for Results

All life processes are sequential. This implies that their various stages must occur in the right order, so much so that if one stage is left out the succeeding stages will not occur, or will occur imperfectly. It also implies that each stage must occur in the spatio-temporal environment or field to which behavior at that stage is adaptive.

Edward Goldsmith, *The Way*

To see an event in its larger context implies a larger punctuation in space and time. The context also gives the events meaning. The situation of two men hitting each other carries a different meaning in a boxing arena than at a management meeting. Nodding one's head means "yes" in the United States and "no" in Albania.

The order of influences is of utmost importance. Strategy processes start at the top. Ownership of an environmental strategy should be established at the board level before it is established at the middle management level. Motivation to learn comes before a seminar on managerial techniques. Checking the reaction to an advertising campaign with market representatives comes before the campaign is launched. Strategic direction is established before reorganization, which comes before competence enhancement programs. The 3rd order problem-solving process (to be discussed in Chapter 15), negotiation (see Chapter 5), and feedback (see Chapter 8) all show that the order of things is of utmost importance.

The number of links the information passes through is also of importance. For each link, the message is interpreted and changed, before being passed on. The message reaching a sales consultant, for example, originally delivered from the CEO to the sales director, can be unrecognizable after passing through all the intermediate links.

Stage of development also should be considered. An organization in the first entrepreneur stage usually needs less management and less motivational activities than at later stages. After some years, initiatives to maintain vitality and to limit bureaucracy are often critical.

A PROJECT FOR QUALITY CERTIFICATION STAGNATES

In this example I shall consider a company in the engineering industry. In order to obtain quality certification, the management decided to start a quality certification program involving the entire company. An external firm of consultants assisted by drawing up a detailed plan for the project. A pro forma information letter was sent to the unions, and the program was started straight away. The workshop was in a tight, competitive market, and the management felt that quality certification would give an important competitive advantage.

However, the program encountered serious problems during implementation. Work on the quality program was continually given lower priority than more pressing problems in production. Even with meticulous follow-up, the plan was not realized. The situation was discussed at a management meeting attended by members of the union. The following hypothesis was agreed on.

Resistance to the implementation was caused by the fact that the employees had not been informed about the overriding purpose of quality certification. Consequently, the value of competitive advantage had not been understood. There was no knowledge of the strategic objectives, the strategic market situation, or other elements which would put it into relief. That other activities were given a higher priority was taken as an expression of the wish to maintain a high level of productivity and quality of work, rather than waste time on pro forma activities.

Based on this understanding, the management decided to stop the program for the time being. An extensive program was started to market the strategy in the organization. Working groups across the organization were given the task of developing parts of the strategy. Thereafter the management prepared a strategy document which was distributed throughout the company and discussed at different meetings. In this strategy document, the gaining of quality certification was rated as a strategic goal. It was placed on line with the other strategic goals and emphasized as a key element. The task of implementing quality control was then restarted according to the original plan. It was completed after a short period without any significant difficulties.

Axiom I.6: Conditions for Results

Optimum effects of influences, external and internal, on ecosystems or organizations are dependent on:

—Whether the element which is influenced is a core element or not
—The context
—The order in which the influences appear
—The number of links the influences pass through
—The stage of development of the system.

In all organizational change, choice of element to influence, context, order of influences, number of links, and stage of development should be taken into consideration, to prevent resistance and to attain optimum results relative to the efforts.

In the above case, the management wanted to push through a program of quality certification. Yet, the process was continually given lower priority in favor of more immediate, value-creating activities. The hypothesis that was reached suggested that this was not a result of conscious sabotage, but of lack of information on the importance of the certification. In other words, the actions were presented to the employees and the middle management outside any meaningful context. The decision to postpone the action until the strategy process was completed gave the desired results. In relation to the above-mentioned principle, this can be understood in three different ways: Quality certification was placed in its proper *context* and thereby became meaningful, or: The presentation of the certification work before the strategy work reflected presentation in the *wrong order*, or: The system reached a new *stage of maturity* through the strategy process. Whatever the reason, the hypothesis gave rise to an efficient solution.

NONLINEARITY

Nonlinearity refers to the phenomenon of living systems not always following predictable or linear paths. A population that has grown steadily for some years may suddenly decrease. A steady improvement of performance may change abruptly for better or for worse. In the world of living organisms, man included, simple, mechanical linearity is not always the rule.

Colloquially, this principle can be restated by the popular saying, "Little strokes fell great oaks." Or, the other way around: "Much ado about nothing." The "fact" that the more you invest in change, the greater change you achieve is questionable. It is more a question of finding the element or key factor that can effect change. In principle, the potential for human and organizational change lies in three different areas: motivation, competence, and organization. From experience, it is the organization either in the form of an organization chart or a work-flow diagram, which is more easily addressed when improvements are required. But should the key to a solution lie in one of the other two areas, either in motivation or competence, then even the most concerted efforts will be futile.

On the other hand, one should be aware of the fact that even a small influence can cause big changes. An example is a company that was going to install a new timekeeping system. In an informal situation the CEO let slip the following humorous comment: "Yes, and now we will even be able to know when you go to the toilet." This small comment resulted in serious consequences for the organization. Massive protests were made about the new timekeeping system. In the negotiations with the unions, there were threats of strike action if the system was not stopped. The same timekeeping system that had been successfully installed in numerous other organizations in cooperation with the unions and management after this event could not be implemented here.

According to systems theory, the potential for high-energy effect as a result of low-energy influence depends on the systems' stability. That is to say, unstable systems change more, and more easily. This conforms with the general knowledge that crisis creates a climate for change. A system in crisis is unstable. An implication of course is: "If you want to change something, create a crisis." When things go well, there is danger. Create an impression of overwhelming danger, and the willingness to change is accelerated.

COMPETENCE DEVELOPMENT IMPROVES PRODUCTIVITY

A pharmaceutical company called in an external consultant to evaluate the status of the company. The company had been in decline over a three-year period. Turnover had dropped by approximately 10%, while the total market had increased by approximately 15%. The productivity was the lowest in the industry.

When the situation was discussed at senior management meetings, attention was repeatedly drawn to the organization chart. Work flow, routines, and reporting were also discussed. They always found details to improve in these areas. Willingness and the ability to implement improvements were evidently good. What was surprising was that all the improvements failed to bring significant results. The consultant reviewed earlier reports and found that a series of reorganizations had been made during the past three to five years. Production and reporting routines, and the general flow of information had been changed over and over again. The external consultant drew up and presented the following hypothesis to the CEO.

Ill-will and willful sabotage were not the reasons for the lack of improvement in productivity. The reason was simple. The actions were directed to the wrong area. Further investigation and analysis in the organization revealed substantial shortcomings in interpersonal skills at all levels of management.

The consultant's proposals were as follows: No further reorganization was to be undertaken during the coming year. Instead, all resources allocated to organizational development were to be utilized in raising the level of skills at all management levels. The competence development program covered interpersonal and management skills. A management information system was to be established solely to monitor the development of competence. Amongst other things, appraisal meetings were to be implemented at all management levels. By this means, the development of competence could be followed up and evaluated, and new objectives set for development.

After one year, productivity had improved by 25%. This was partly due to environmental changes and partly due to the internal developmental program. An organizational review could now be undertaken, since substantial resources had been liberated within the organization.

CHECK YOUR COMPANY: CONDITIONS FOR RESULTS

- Do managers take context into consideration when they make plans?
- Do they take order of influences into account?
- Do they bear stage of development in mind?
- Is the number of links that any message passes through reduced to a minimum?
- Are core elements searched for when changes are planned?
- Are managers aware that "good times" are the most dangerous for the company?

CHECK YOURSELF: CONDITIONS FOR RESULTS

- Apply the above on yourself.

Chapter 11

Function Replacement to Prevent Resistance

> With elegance and economy, nature subordinates means to end. Matter is for the sake of form, and both are for the sake of operation. Every cell, every tissue, every organ serves a purpose. Every animal, every plant directs its activities to an end. The whole of nature is ordered by purpose.
>
> Robert Augros and George Stanciu, *The New Biology*

When pesticides came, optimism was great. Insect pests would be destroyed, and great leaps lay ahead for civilization. The lesson was hard to learn: The insect pests had a *function* in the ecosystem, as food for birds and as spreaders of pollen. Their function in this web either had to be replaced or the use of pesticides had to be stopped, or at least restricted. Even species and behavior that seem to have no value turn out to have a function in the system of which they are a part.

A real-life example from the context of business should illustrate this further: A management group in a small enterprise spent many hours every week in management meetings. A business consultant made a remark to the director, proposing that this activity could be reduced by 50%. The basis for his suggestion was a comparison with similar organizations. The director took an initiative, and over a period of two months the activity in fact was reduced by about 50%. This situation lasted for another two months, after which the meeting activity steadily increased again. Soon the management group was back where it started, "because of an extraordinary situation." This situation was no more extraordinary, however, than that the meeting frequency retained its high level after the "extraordinary situation" was brought to an end.

A half year later, the consultant again turned up in the office, and learned what had happened. Together with the director he made a diagnosis: The frequent and long-lasting meetings had a hidden *function*. Since this had not been replaced, the group had returned to the old regime. The function, they found out, was to serve as a forum for mutual support and reduce anxiety in the management group. It turned out they had not formulated, nor even discussed, management philosophy in the group. Further, they had no strategic direction or common basis for their work. To replace the frequent and long meetings, and still take care of their function, they decided to put some effort into developing a solid management philosophy, and also started a simple process of strategy development and leadership. After four months of this activity, the amount and length of the management meetings were again reduced, and this time the reduction was permanent.

Identifying possible function replacement follows this simple pattern:

Model for identifying function replacement:
1. Describe the element/activity to be replaced.
2. Map all the functions of this element/activity.
3. Decide on ways of taking care of this function other than through the original element/activity.

Our management group mentioned above fit the pattern like this:

1. Frequent and long-lasting meetings.
2. Mutual support, lowering of anxiety.
3. Development of management philosophy; development of strategic plan.

Quitting smoking is a popular sport. An essential part of the quit-smoking regime is to identify possible replacement of its function, as for example:

1. Smoking 30 cigarettes a day.
2. Relaxation.
3. Deep relaxation techniques/knitting/drinking tea/jogging.

Another way of stating this process is to see it as hierarchy of means and ends:

1. Define the element/activity to be replaced as means.

2. Define the ends of these means.

3. Develop other means leading to the same ends.

This pattern equals the one demonstrated in Chapter 2 (Figure 2.4) and Chapter 5 (Figure 5.1).

A 10% INCREASE IN PRODUCTIVITY

A production and sales company in the field of electronics experienced strong price competition over a period of time. Margins dropped by an average of 6% per year over the time span of three years. The management found that total productivity would have to be increased by 10% within two years. If not, the company would be in serious trouble. In the depressed market, an increase in turnover was deemed to be unrealistic. It was clear to the management that reducing manpower was the means by which the increase of productivity could best be realized.

External consultants were used to establish the potential for improvement. Sizeable potentials were identified, and measures were instigated. However, the actions were executed without enthusiasm at midmanagement and production levels, and in the sales teams. Reporting was inaccurate and partially incorrect. The management reviewed the situation after four months. All implemented actions were reasonable and sensible, but results were simply not forthcoming. The following hypothesis was formulated.

All actions were being subconsciously sabotaged by the employees. They realized that redundancies would be necessary in order to achieve the improvement in productivity. There was every possibility that colleagues would end up in unemployment, owing to the current labor market situation. "Resistance" toward the measures was not an expression of reluctance, but expressed a wish to protect colleagues from unemployment. Based on this understanding, it was decided to adopt a completely fresh approach. An extensive project was started. This program offered training so that employees could be transferred within the organization. Some would be offered redundancy payment. Comprehensive inquiries were made at other companies to arrange possible reemployment. An outplacement consultant was also engaged. Actions directed toward productivity improvements were implemented concurrently with the planned redundancies, and followed up closely. Within a two-year period, the company achieved an improvement in productivity of more than 10%.

Axiom I.7: Function Replacement

All components in an ecosystem have a function. All behavior in an organization carries functions. If the components or the behavior are changed or removed, the more essential functions should be replaced, to maintain stability.

In all organizational change, an analysis of the functions of the elements to be changed should be performed. These should be analyzed from the first, second, and third positions, and important functions should be replaced, to prevent resistance and to reach optimum results.

The hypothesis which explained why it was so difficult to achieve a 10% increase in productivity in this production organization was as follows: Implementation of the actions was prevented by an unconscious and hidden solidarity with those who would lose their jobs as a result of the improvement in productivity. Only when this consideration was taken into account could the necessary measures be taken.

This principle opens the way for a series of hypotheses when considering change in organizations. Even activities such as office gossip, backchat, low efficiency, and so on can have a function. As soon as we have a well-founded hypothesis as to what function the behavior serves, there are possibilities of finding a replacement. If the function is replaced, the potential result is a change with minimum resistance. In other words, we can understand resistance in this context as being an expression of the wish to maintain a function.

At community level, environmentalists need the concept of function replacement. If vital functions, for example work places, are lost through greenery, there is great risk of setbacks. An ecological strategy for community development has to answer the questions of function replacements.

CHECK YOUR COMPANY: FUNCTION REPLACEMENT

- Are functions and their replacement considered in decision making?
- Does the management check for hidden functions before changes are implemented?

CHECK YOURSELF: FUNCTION REPLACEMENT

- Apply the questions above to yourself as a manager.
- When you want to make personal changes, do you tend to think in terms of *stopping* an ongoing activity or in terms of *starting* new and different activities?

Part III

Ancient Man in Modern Organizations

There are one hundred and ninety-three species of large and small apes. One hundred and ninety-two of them are furry. The exception is a naked ape which has given himself the name Homo Sapiens. This peculiar and very prosperous species spends a large part of his time inquiring into his noble motives, and just as much time carefully disregarding the basic motives. . . . He is bragging, intensely in search of new discoveries, represents a perilously numerous species, and it is time that we investigate his fundamental behavior.

Desmond Morris, *The Naked Ape* [author's translation]

Chapter 12

Territories

> The danger, that in one part of the available biotope, a too huge amount of one species should assemble, so that all means of subsistence be exhausted and the animals starve, while other parts of the area stay unused, is best averted by animals of the same species repulsing each other.
>
> Konrad Lorenz, *On Aggression* [author's translation]

We are now moving from the *metaphor* of ecosystems to the reality of ancient man. The concepts from ethology, the science of animal behavior, as applied in this part of the book, should be taken *literally*. Man *is* a territorial creature, he *forms* hierarchies, and he *possesses* the properties described in the areas of motivation and problem solving. He is fitted to a niche, and problems arise when his natural environment disappears. His fitness is then reduced, and this represents a threat to his well-being. It seems to be both valid and important to maintain this perspective, even on man-made organizations. But this does not rule out the valuable concepts from sociology, social anthropology, and psychology, for example. These disciplines shed light on the differences and idiosyncrasies of organizational cultures and behavioral patterns. At the same time, natural science provides many concepts by which to understand the common, and not least the irrational aspects.

In this part of the book I shall take Desmond Morris, cited on the previous page, literally. By doing that, I raise a controversial perspective. Some people seem to feel that seeing man as just another species implies degrading Homo Sapiens. I disagree. The intention, or even the content of the following chapters, is not to be regarded as contradicting a perspective of man as a spiritual being, or man as a rational being. Man can be spiritual, man can be rational, and man obviously can be "an animal." To deny this aspect is to give away core knowledge of value for our understanding of even modern man. I prefer to see the spiritual, rational, and biological aspects of man as complementary, not exclusive. Man as a biological species should not be set against man as a cultural being. I regard the traditional antagonisms between social and natural sciences to be unproductive. Man is a biological being, he has inborn characteristics, he is not a "black box." His biological patterns are shaped by culture, and he is culturally very shapable. Both of these perspectives contribute to a better understanding of his behavior. However, in this part of the book I shall focus primarily on man's biological being.

A COMMUNICATION BREAKDOWN
IN CORPORATE MANAGEMENT

I should like to start the discussion of man's territoriality with a story from real life. This happened in the top management group of a corporation. In this case the corporate management was comprised of a CEO and seven division managers. The manager of the most successful division saw his suggestions, statements, and contributions to general discussions repudiated by the CEO over and over again. He described the situation at a confidential meeting with a personal advisor who, in turn, offered the following hypothesis: The division manager was a relatively young man who had made excellent progress in his career. In many ways he epitomized "the new age," with a progressive management style and a dynamic, fearless attitude. The CEO was a member of the old school. The constant repudiation was seen to be an expression of the CEO feeling his position threatened. The proposals and general style of the division manager were experienced as being an invasion of the CEO's territory, built up over a long period of time.

The advisor suggested the following: The division manager should establish more frequent, direct contact with the CEO *outside* meetings. The division manager should familiarize himself with the traditions and history of the organization. As far as possible, he should formulate his proposals using terms and references associated with these traditions. He should present his proposals, first and foremost, in face-to-face situations. In cases where the CEO put forward the manager's proposals as if they were his own, the division manager should support them without appearing to try to take the credit for them. Finally, the advisor suggested showing restraint in corporate meetings, making sure that the division manager's proposals are propounded by others. He could also present proposals himself, but then more as questions, or suggestions, or as stories about "things which other organizations have implemented to good effect."

The division manager decided to follow the suggestions made by the advisor. After six months he achieved the following changes: The CEO often contacted him to ask for advice; and he also frequently asked him for his opinion at the management meetings. The division manager had been able to implement substantial changes that also had inspired changes in divisions other than his own. On the whole, communication in the corporate management team as such was greatly improved. How is this to be understood?

In systems of living organisms, different forms of "strife and rivalry" regulate territories, mating rights, and hierarchical positions. It is difficult for some people to accept that members of a civilized society are subject to these "primitive" principles. Yet, the ability to recognize territoriality is an asset. And it opens up for unexpected solutions. It could have been tempting for the division manager to see the CEO's behavior as stubborn, cruel, and conservative, or that he had other negative characteristics. Such an understanding would naturally have led him to "fight the good fight" for reason against unreasonableness, or for the new against the old.

Instead, we can understand this as being a natural phenomenon, where there is a hierarchical position or territory to defend from the start. The adherent of the old school had an established territory which, unknown to himself, he was trying to defend against intruders. By not threatening the CEO, and respecting the traditions, a "common territory" was created. In this new situation, cooperation could proceed undisturbed and the CEO was even able to ask the division manager for help on difficult issues without losing face.

In this manner, professional rivalry, interdepartmental competition, power games, and so on can be seen in a different light. Irrational behavior often can be interpreted as being an expression of natural processes which we must relate to in a constructive manner.

TERRITORIALITY

We see from the above that the insight into this part of man's mentality really is of help. Rivalry between professions, between neighbors, between departments in organizations, stands forth in a new light. Man's territoriality is of a more encompassing character, however, than it is for other beings. The reason is man's symbolic abilities. While animal territoriality centers mainly around physical objects, man can exhibit territoriality connected to abstract phenomena. Territorial behavior can defend a viewpoint, a policy, a strategy, a religion, and more. In fact, any disagreement may have associated aspects of territoriality! To illustrate with an example: A senior medical consultant was appointed to run a hospital department.

After a couple of weeks he put forward a plan on how the department could best be changed, together with a draft program for implementation. This caused a serious conflict, especially among the nurses. All the proposals had to be withdrawn. The medical consultant decided to leave the department shortly afterward. He met the ward sister again at a seminar, two years later. They were then able to sum up: They agreed that nearly all the proposals he had suggested at the time were good ones. Some of them were in fact now being practiced in the department. But, coming from him, the proposals were totally impossible to accept. There were two reasons for this. First, he was a newcomer, and thereby an intruder into their territory. Second, he was a doctor, thereby representing "a rivaling tribe."

We must not take a pessimistic view on this. Rather, I regard it as an advantage to be aware of this pattern, as in our story from corporate management. Even at a more general level, territoriality should not be seen as utterly negative behavior. Among others, Konrad Lorenz, the famous ethologist, has proposed that intraspecific territoriality should be seen mainly as an ordering principle. Its function is to spread the population over a sufficiently large area, to give enough space for each individual for survival. He also pointed out that the aggression exhibited as a main rule is not of a destructive or deadly character. In fact, it should be seen as a constructive force, contributing to the survival of the species.[1]

Territoriality among humans in modern civilizations in general, and in modern business organizations especially, can be destructive or constructive. But to act as if it does not exist would not be wise. Territoriality has strong positive potentials: The definition of a common territory for all employees strengthens the feeling of all employees as being a "we." Also, it brings down the strife between groups and individuals to a minimum. A common territory is built through common strategy ownership processes, the building of a common language and culture, common activities, and so forth. Through these activities, territoriality becomes a tremendous force for the success of the company. At the same time, the territories of individuals, groups, departments, and so on need to be defined. This defining of subterritories in the organization should not be too strong. If it is, territoriality between groups or individuals inside the organization will take on a destructive character. But some definition is necessary, to give the codex for areas of responsibility, authority, and accountability.

It should be admitted, however, that territoriality can take on a destructive character. It is really a hidden pattern of great strength. For instance, in a situation of reorganization it is easy to catch. You may recognize the scene: The managers of finance, market, and sales all claim, on an "objective" basis, that *their* department should have more professionals, higher wages, and more authority. A diffuse, double communication then is going on. The arguments are real, but even more real is the force behind the "objective" standpoint: territoriality *par excellence*. As in this case, when territoriality is about real territories it is extraordinarily strong. In fact, it is so strong that a lasting, good process leading up to consensus often cannot be counted on. For this reason, reorganization often has to be carried out through a "clean cut" from top.

From a third position, and seen through the filter of ethology, management meetings can be an entertaining occurrence. Most managers are totally unaware of the stream of communication signals, verbal and nonverbal, of a territorial kind. Even in strict, businesslike meetings, rarely as much as 50% of the attention is focused on the case at hand. The rest is spent on the hidden games of territoriality, or its relative—hierarchical behavior.[2]

This supplements our understanding of the difficulties of providing help across cultures. Even the best help is again and again repelled, often for reasons of territoriality. At an unconscious level, the help is perceived as intrusion or as humiliating. To maintain a feeling of identity, territoriality is activated. This is one key to the understanding of such reactions. The other lies in our concept of the hierarchy of system levels. The larger punctuation, in many situations of international aid practice, shows a situation where the helper is really the one who profits, while the receiver of help is the loser. Under these overriding conditions, grateful compliance with the helper can hardly be expected.

Why do humans so often turn down good advice? Why do 1st order processes of change as a general rule foster more resistance than 2nd order processes do, and 2nd order more than 3rd order? A significant part of the answer is territoriality. 1st order implies that someone from outside the territory comes in and gives the order. This is met with defense of territory, be that territory a physical one, or a symbolic "identity," or "privacy." 2nd order implies someone setting premises in the other's territory, again leading to territoriality. 3rd order implies making a common territory, inside which "we" will collaborate. Territoriality can then be channelled toward "our" common objectives.

The concept of territoriality, then, applies to all scenes of interhuman relations. It has implications for organizations and interhuman communication in any situation where humans interact.

A NOTE ON HUMAN MOTIVATION

The understanding of motives is essential for any business. What makes humans do what they do, and with what degree of commitment, is the domain of motivational psychology. As a general rule, business has taken a very simple standpoint on this area: Pay a co-worker more and he will perform better. But the picture is complicated by several traits that are typical of man.

Even with chimpanzees, experiments show that the animals may choose, for example, the opportunity to explore an interesting environment at the cost of receiving material rewards like food and drink. This may happen even if the animal is thirsty and hungry. The motive of exploration, even for chimpanzees then, can be stronger than the motives of eating and drinking.

A very interesting experiment was performed with preschool children. The children were given the opportunity to paint. One group was rewarded with coins for painting, the other not. As expected, the group who got coins painted more. This was the case, however, only as long as reward was kept up. When it was taken away, the children who had been rewarded for painting painted significantly *less* than the children who had never received any external reward for this behavior. The children who had received coins possibly perceived the situation like this: "Painting must be boring, since we have to get paid to perform it," while the other children would think: "Painting is fun."[3]

The experiment is illustrative, because of the fact that man reacts to what he perceives, not to reality. This even goes for medical treatment. Experiments have provided an overwhelming documentation of the tremendous force of the placebo effect, that is, the part of medical effectiveness generated by belief and not by chemical influence.[4] The perceptual meaning of enhanced payment decides its effect. Since different cultures attribute a different meaning to events, any motivational effect of differing rewards will vary. For example, let us look at payment as motivating factor. As long as increased payment is new, it is perceived as "higher than usual," and it has a reinforcing effect. But after some months it is not "new" or "different" anymore, and the reinforcing effect is lost. In fact, a negative motivational potential is established. The payment is perceived as a matter of course, and not receiving it may lead to demotivation.

Let us give an example of how mechanistic thinking may turn out in this area: A firm of stevedores in Holland handles the cargo of large freighters. One of the main activities of the work force is to unload containers with the help of cranes and forklift trucks. The management worked out a new payment system, the aim of which was increased productivity. The system was based on piecework: The workers' wages were calculated on the basis of the number of containers off-loaded and stacked. The workers had previously operated on a fixed wage system. To its surprise, the management experienced that within fourteen days, productivity had sunk by 20%. The psychosocial climate within the company had deteriorated dramatically. The reason was that the employees perceived the changes as an expression of distrust. They were not consulted or involved in the establishment of the new system. Soon after, piecework was withdrawn, but it took a long time before the climate at the company returned to normal.

In spite of these variations, can we find some common cultural, motivational categories applicable to archaic man? Let us leave out the general basic needs for food, water, and sex, and the general need for air, and warmth, and see man as a social being. Acceptance by a group and belonging to a group are of considerable value to him. Group norms usually override the effect of material rewards.[5]

Evolutionary theory has had a tendency to underline competition and aggression at the cost of cooperation. But man, more than being a lone ranger, is typically a flock animal. Obviously, motivation attached to this aspect is strong. The willingness to contribute to the common best, and even to contribute to humans outside their own group, is a strong motivational force among humans. For instance, if a price tag were to be put on all the voluntary work done, for scouts, the Red Cross, sports clubs, and AA, to mention but a few, the calculated GNP would make a significant leap upward. Cooperation and altruism are significant motivational factors for man.

The dichotomy of human nature, that is, egoism versus altruism, is well illustrated in the problems of the commons. If a human system of any size shares a common good, egoism draws in the direction of "PP-CC," that is, privatize profit and commonize costs.[6] The personal profit is immediate, surveyable and reinforcing; the negative effects of drawing too heavily on the common resources are long-term and cannot be surveyed. Our archaic cause-and-effect thinking and our motivational egoism work toward a too-heavy exploitation of common resources, with the resulting long-term draining or destruction of the commons. However, there are obvious counterforces. Such forces are the decisions and institutionalization of common regulatory rules. In ancient societies these often took the form of religious rules, rituals, and beliefs. Other factors are the personal relations or kinship between the people who draw on the commons and the surveyability of the consequences for society as a whole. We see how this fits the thesis of local production for local consumption for local recirculation. Surveyability and personal relations are stronger in smaller units. The upholding and reestablishment of common rules and beliefs is more probable in smaller communities.

Taxation of international commons presents a very difficult challenge. Recent years have shown how difficult even the topic of whaling is, for example, although the economic implications of whaling are marginal. This is a good illustration of how destructive territoriality between nations can be when it enters the arena, when egoism overrides altruism, and when surveyability, personal relations, degree of kinship, and established or institutionalized common rules are all weak.

GROUP STRENGTHENING

A common contribution toward common goals is the single most effective way in which man strengthens his group. It is something all parents know: If the children engage in destructive quarrels, give them something common to work for.[7] The establishment of governing common goals, values, and actions seems to be a key to a positive channelling of the biological forces inborn in man.

Axiom II.1: Territoriality

Humans establish and defend territories in nature and in organizations, through:

—Common contributions to governing goals
—Contrasting themselves with other groups
—Developing group symbols, rituals, and communication
—Developing common rules and beliefs

Governing common goals, values, symbols, and actions should be established to provide a common territory and identity, and a sound motivational climate in the organization.

Another well-known social pattern is the phenomenon of finding an external enemy. It seems as if man's tendency to think in "either-or" patterns makes him feel that "if they are bad, then we are good." This goes for the children's games of "we are friends and we are the good ones. We will not let those others into our group, they are silly and bad." This also applies between nations and cultures. In this light, prejudice has an important function: It helps "us" to feel good, since "they" are bad. In companies, negative stories about the competitors, their ethics, service, and products are a significant form of social cement for the group. Enemy-images serve the same function. For instance, it is an open question whether cannibalism is a real phenomenon to any extent, or is a projection of an archaic fantasy on the part of others. Whatever the answer, reports on cannibalism are typically delivered by people who have not actually witnessed its practice themselves, but have met someone who knows someone who has. In our context, it suffices to say that any constructions of enemy-images, or even less dramatic stories about the others is a means of strengthening one's own group.

Anthropologists have given a well of descriptions of symbols and rituals that keep communities and groups together. Industrial "rational" man often misses the parallel to his own activities. Be it a military unit, a football team, or a corporate unit, the uniforms, signs, rituals, and rules for in-group behavior all are present there. These, of course, are not at all "rational," they are instinctive, deeply rooted behavioral patterns that strengthen the group. A whole set of "truths" also develops over time. These become embedded in language and become invisible presuppositions shared by the group.

Some very "rational" leaders do not like these traits of man, and try to defeat their existence. But this pays badly. As a territorial being, man also exhibits characteristic patterns of group strengthening. If these are not taken into consideration and channelled in a constructive manner, they take on a life of their own. The risk of mean manifestations, such as discrimination against minorities and interdepartmental strife, thereby increases.

CHECK YOUR COMPANY: TERRITORIALITY

- Are common goals, values, symbols, and actions established?
- Are territories clearly defined for persons and groups?
- Is territoriality stronger for the whole enterprise than for the singular parts?
- Are company symbols and rituals well established?
- Are motivational potentials of both egoistic and altruistic nature utilized?
- Are initiatives across lines and levels welcomed?

CHECK YOURSELF: TERRITORIALITY

- Apply the questions above to yourself.
- Do you appreciate other managers' involvement in your sphere of authority?
- Do you easily let other people get the credit for common achievements?
- How easily do you accept an outsider's view as valid?

Chapter 13

Hierarchies

> Members of a species fight amongst themselves for two very good reasons: either to assert themselves in a social hierarchy, or to assert their territorial claims. . . .
>
> Desmond Morris, *The Naked Ape* [author's translation]

Hierarchies in organizations are a much disputed phenomenon. It is popular to regard them as old-fashioned and less worthy than flat structures, networks, and so on. I believe that these disputes often miss the target. Hierarchies *are* a fact, just as is territoriality. It is nothing to argue for or against. A hierarchy is established in any situation with more than one human being gathered in an organized setting. This might become clearer if we include the concept of "roles." Social psychology has shown again and again that in a group of people who have to perform a particular task, the members immediately and unconsciously adopt different roles. Some take on an active role, some a passive; some a creative, some a realistic. Some will be the leaders, some the followers. After a very short time a hierarchy is established, based on such roles.

If the hierarchy is not made explicit, it will still exist, but in an informal way. This is actually the general experience from "flat organizations." They are formally flat, and informally hierarchical. From a biological point of view, we can ask, as we did in the case of territoriality, what natural function may this hierarchy have? A good answer is that it is economizing. It spreads functions, which provides a possibility to specialize and thereby economize. Everybody doing everything is less economical than everybody doing his part. It also opens up for decision making without everyone participating. This gives flexibility. It also functions as a kind of "evolutionary pressure" in the organization, motivating for better performance to reach higher up. This serves as a constructive force in a homeotelic organization.

A GOVERNMENT INSTITUTION WITH POOR SERVICE

The importance of a clear hierarchy is illustrated by this example: The institution concerned carried out administrative activities that directly affected a significant number of people and indirectly affected the infrastructure of the community. A market survey revealed unacceptable processing times and numerous examples of unacceptable customer service within the institution. The organization was granted funds to pay for assistance from consultants over a three-year period.

The organization was characterized by strong ideals of equality. Its first CEO had been an advocate of the flat organization and of company democracy. After he left, the institution had grown to more than one thousand employees. Yet, it was still expected that all information on operations, changes in administrative routines, and social conditions affecting the institution should be discussed and decided on by all employees.

The organization was also characterized by strong disputes between colleagues and struggles for power. There were an extortionate number of meetings, which were frequently long and fruitless. For this reason, frustration within the organization was high, and measures of improvement were frequently discussed. The management, however, was unable to break the vicious circle.

An extensive organizational development program was started at the suggestion of the external consultants. The program, which included strengthening the principle that all information should be spread within the organization, was well received by most of the employees. Most of them would participate in the development of an action plan in different ways. A major competence development program would also be started.

The program was evaluated after one year, and it was concluded that it had not resulted in any positive changes. A new survey showed a slight worsening in the market's evaluation of the institution. In addition, it seemed that the internal frustration had increased. The external consultants, the management, and representatives of the authorities sat down to reach an understanding of the situation, and arrived at the following hypothesis.

The intercolleague rivalry and the power struggles were an expression of individual attempts to establish a hierarchy where none existed. The general frustration and the cry for more information and participation should be understood as an expression of a need to clarify which decisions were valid, positions in the hierarchy, and to establish generally clearer guidelines. A dramatic program of change was started.

The program entailed a change in all reporting routines. All questions had to go through the official channels. Information was changed and adapted to the needs of the different levels and departments. All meetings that did not have clear objectives were banned. Different management levels negotiated meeting quotas which could not be exceeded without the CEO's permission. Time frames were fixed for all meetings. Only competence development which had already been agreed to could be followed through. Also, for the first time in the history of the organization, consequential action was implemented when the activities one was assigned, or had responsibility for, were not carried out.

The measures brought a wave of protest and resistance. The union representatives who had been used to going directly to whatever levels they wanted to were referred to the person responsible. All resulting meetings with the unions were subject to strict time and agenda restrictions. Within two months the program led to a potential strike. Twice-weekly status meetings between senior management, representatives of the authorities, and the consultants were held during this period.

After this the climate slowly improved. After a year and a half the situation was satisfactory. The time allocated to meetings was reduced by 30%. The market perceived service to have improved by approximately 20%, and, on average, processing lead times were halved. The majority of the routines implemented a year and a half earlier had been formally removed by then, but were still being followed. Let us again formulate our learning as an axiom.

Axiom II.2: Hierarchies

Humans establish hierarchical groups and/or communities.
An unambiguous, formal hierarchy should be established and supported to prevent hierarchy-related strife in the organization.

The cure that this operation went through was not painless. The reestablishment of a hierarchy is often experienced as being undemocratic, infringing on personal liberty, and even degrading. Yet, I conclude that in general a clear hierarchy is best for the social climate in the long run.

This axiom should not be interpreted as a defense for the old, rigid, line organization. Broad, horizontal communications and cooperation, and organization of projects appear to be indispensable to progressive companies that are successful in implementing change. But I believe specifically that it is the structured hierarchy, with clearly defined areas of responsibility and authority, that makes flexible functioning possible. To conclude, it should not be a case of *either* hierarchy *or* project organization, of either hierarchy or network organization, of either hierarchy or team organization. It should be a case of *"and,"* not *"or."*

We have seen that struggles for hierarchical positions may be caused by a lack of hierarchy or by a lack of common goals, as in heterotelic organizations. Bad management constitutes a third category. Organizations in this situation spontaneously struggle to establish a working hierarchy as a substitute for one that is not functioning. This is too often perceived as an unwanted uproar from the lower ranks. Instead, it should be taken as valid information that it is time for a serious evaluation of the management concerned. Prevention of negative strife in this category is possible. A key condition has to do with the basis for appointments to managerial positions. Appointments should be based primarily on managerial competence. Time of service in the company and professional competence in other areas than management should come second, and personal relations should be regarded as irrelevant.

From the point of view of human systems, hierarchical struggles should be seen as efforts to establish good hierarchical order where this is lacking. Thus seen, they have obvious positive aspects. Mere passive submission to no hierarchy or bad hierarchies is a symptom of organizational illness. Hierarchical struggles, then, give hope for healing.

CHECK YOUR COMPANY: HIERARCHIES

• Do responsibility, authority, and accountability overlap for all positions?
• Are advancements primarily based on relevant competence and performance?
• How common is bypassing in communication across levels?
• Is one person appointed as responsible for any task in the company?

CHECK YOURSELF: HIERARCHIES

• Apply the questions above to yourself.

Chapter 14

Ecologically Sound
Working Environments

> If man has existed for two million years, then his experience as an industrialist is not more than two days in the life of a man of seventy, in fact quite negligible.
>
> Edward Goldsmith, "Adam and Eve Revisited"

Since the 1950s, business and industry in industrialized countries have focused to an increasing extent on people as being the company's most important resource. Good work places, not only physically good, but also psychologically and socially good, are an essential to the company. But what makes a work place into a good work place? Here I shall outline a theory, viewed from an ecological perspective and making a further contribution to our general ecological approach to business and industry.

The main premise for such a theory is as follows: Biologically speaking, people today are practically identical to those from tens of thousands of years ago. Through evolution, Homo Sapiens has adapted to an existence as hunter or collector. Man formed nomadic groups and tribes which wandered the wild and almost limitless plains. He was shaped then for a lifestyle, an ecological niche, qualitatively rather different from that of today, not least from life in the industrialized countries. What implications does this have for life in the company?

As an introduction to answering this question, let us pay a visit to a zoo: Large felines wander restlessly around, confined to a few square meters. They gnaw at their paws and show all the typical signs of stress and neurosis. Apathetic animals that are used to running free, isolated animals used to living in flocks, aggressive and frightened birds, all show that something is wrong. Or let us go to a fish farm. Literally tons of antibiotics have to be fed to the salmon in order to keep disease and epidemics at bay. *Stress and illness increase when the difference between the organisms' actual life environment (modern industrial society/zoo/fish farm) on the one hand, and its natural niche on the other hand, becomes too large.*

Large cultural differences in lifestyle and individual "inhuman" achievements have led many people to underestimate this factor. But the fact that we are enormously adaptable should not blind us to the limits of our biology. A human being presumably cannot jump longer than ten meters. He can process about 10,000 mental signals per second, not 20,000. Our short-term memory can store approximately seven figures, names, or impressions, not fourteen. Man has limitations set by his biological equipment, and we do best in acknowledging and respecting this.

Can the common factors of good work places be understood in the light of ecological theory? I think this is possible and shall suggest that it be formulated as follows.

Axiom II.3: Man's Natural Environment

Humans, by evolution, are adapted to environments giving opportunity to:

—enjoy natural physiochemical environments
—enjoy broad variations of patterns of movement and tasks
—enjoy varied sensory exposure
—explore, and learn by experience
—obtain an overview of and meaning to their own existence
—enjoy affiliation to a group
—exist in surveyable communities and institutions

Ecologically sound working environments are physiochemically natural, provide opportunity to enjoy different tasks and patterns of movement and varied sensory exposure, opportunity to explore and to learn by experience, overview of and meaning to one's own existence, and social belonging and surveyability.

On this background, let us first examine the *physical* working environment.

Assertion: *Man has adapted to natural surroundings and needs unspoiled nature in his surroundings.* Foul air, chemical pollution, radiation, and noise are all physical factors that create stress among people. Further, architects and civil engineers have a special responsibility to link work places to natural surroundings, or to bring nature inside the building. For instance, why do most of us prefer windows in our offices?[1] It is because they give contact with natural light and a feeling of being free. The less contaminated the physical working environment, and the closer to nature both in interior form and in relation to the surroundings, the more eco-friendly the working environment can be said to be.

Assertion: *Man has adapted to an existence involving variation in patterns of movement and tasks.* Unnatural and strained working positions are major problems. Monotony, especially, causes physical stress. An ecologically sound place of work is arranged to give physical variation. Irrespective of the type of strain, monotony leads to stress: on the assembly line, at the data screen, or at the switchboard. In 1980, 20% of occupational absenteeism in the United states was related to RSI, or Repetitive Stress Injury. By 1992, the share had risen to more than 50%.[2]

Now let us examine the *psychological* working environment.

Assertion: *Man has adapted to an existence with varied sensory influences and the opportunity to investigate and learn from experience.* Pure routine work, monotonous sensory influences, and the acquisition of predigested knowledge by rote induce stress. When routine work has to be done it should be spread among many people, or interspersed by more creative or investigatory tasks.

Assertion: *Man has adapted to an existence where he sees the results of his actions, has an overall view of the entire context in which the action takes place, and where he can be of use to a larger group.* For example, small production groups building a whole car from start to finish represent a more eco-friendly organizing principle than, at the other extreme, the one shown in Chaplin's "Modern Times." A company that informs its employees about the firm's total situation creates a healthier environment than one that gives no information. A company that adds value to products or services and reveals everyone's usefulness in production is more ecologically sound than one that does not.

Finally, let us look at the *social* working environment.

Assertion: *Man has adapted to an existence with affiliation to a group that interrelates for a common purpose.* A company should be organized with a view to developing groups with strong affiliations. The group should experience the reaching of actual targets, and these achievements should be celebrated in some tangible manner. To apply this in the context of greening of business: The hallmark of environmentally oriented companies should be environment-preserving targets set to contribute to our common, better future, and achieved through joint efforts in the group.

Assertion: *Man has adapted to an existence within surveyable communities and social institutions.* An open-door policy, with scope for dialogue and problem solving across organizational levels, should prevail. Bureaucratic "concrete institutions"[3] induce stress. This obviously also includes the question of size. "One hundred people is probably close to the 'designed limit' for human acquaintance—the maximum number of individuals with whom a human being can reasonably interact at more than a superficial level," say Ornstein and Ehrlich.[4] I dare not state the optimum

Table 14.1
Number of Two-person Relationships as a Function of Group Size (Based on
Ornstein & Ehrlich, 1989)

Number of people in group/community	Number of possible two-person relationships
10	45
20	190
100	4,950
1,000	499,500
5,000	12,497,500
15,000	112,492,500

number of people constituting a work group, division, or a company seen
from a human ecological point of view. But we should remember that the
number of possible relationships between people grows exponentially as
the number of people grows arithmetically in a group (see Table 14.1).

What is interesting here is not primarily *what* constitutes a physically,
psychologically, or socially healthy working environment. The main point
is the ecological *reason* why the working environment ought to be as described, and why divergence creates stress. We can thereby turn this reason into an integral part of our ecological understanding. A company with
a high environmental profile should have environmentally friendly internal
working conditions as well.

To avoid possible misunderstandings, I should like to add that the main
purpose here has been to point out a few *complementary*, and not finite,
elements in a general understanding of stress in connection with the working environment. Nor is it the case, of course, that all working environments can be built up from *one* standard base. In addition to the premises
of our biological equipment, we should consider differences in culture.
Changing a well-established, unnatural way of life to a more natural direction can, for instance, be stressful in itself. A New York City resident
may well experience stress the first time he is let loose in a mountain
paradise.

CHECK YOUR COMPANY: WORKING ENVIRONMENT

The Physical Environment

• Is the working environment free of chemical and auditive pollution?

• Do the co-workers enjoy fresh air and natural light?

• Are natural and aesthetic materials used in buildings and the interior?

- Do the co-workers enjoy varied patterns of movement?
- Are work postures natural and varied?

The Psychological Environment

- Do the co-workers participate in varied tasks
- Do they enjoy varied sensory exposure?
- Do they have the opportunity to explore and learn?
- Are they well-informed of the company's overall situation?
- Are they well-informed of the role of their contribution in the total chain of value creation?
- Do they have influence on their own situation?

The Social Environment

- Does everybody belong to a surveyable primary group?
- Are the paths of decisions surveyable and unbureaucratic?
- Do the co-workers have the opportunity to collaborate with others in everyday value creation or in special problem-solving tasks or projects?
- Are social gatherings arranged for?

CHECK YOURSELF: WORKING ENVIRONMENT

- How are your personal conditions regarding the factors mentioned above?

Chapter 15

Thinking and Problem Solving

According to an old joke, making its tired rounds in anthropology departments, the missing link between *apes* and *homo sapiens* has at last been discovered. It turns out to be *man.* . . .
Paul Watzlawick, *Ultra-Solutions or How to Fail Most Successfully*

Ornstein and Ehrlich, in their book *New World New Mind*, hypothesize that we are biased in our thinking because of our evolutionary history.[1] Our thinking is adaptive to a situation with gangs of humans hunting and gathering in untouched nature, with a population of a few thousand spread over the whole globe, with no technology. In this situation our decision making is mainly right and functional. "Catch as much as possible, throw away the garbage and never think of tomorrow." Simple, causal thinking and narrow punctuation had a survival value. Ancient man got more direct feedback from his environment than modern man does. Killing too much game would threaten his existence in the next round. The ecological understanding possessed by many fourth world cultures may be regarded as inherited from ancient man. But as man-made changes in the environment have occurred, it looks as if we must develop new wisdom for our complex time. Maybe our very first step is to admit that such concepts as punctuation, mental filters, and fourth position are of relevance to us.

Our best Western tradition emphasizes objectivity or neutrality when important decisions are to be made. For example, a judge should not be a party in a case. Investigating committees should consist of members with no personal interest in a certain conclusion. In other words, the decision makers should be appointed from outside the system punctuated. Successful peace negotiations often depend on representatives from outside the system in conflict. But who should be appointed when it comes to the international ecological conflicts? Obviously, nobody represents an ideal third party. However unsolvable, the problem should remind us of one thing: When thinking of ecological problems, and especially the global entity, we should be well aware of all our biases. This should induce a self-critical and humble attitude. Industrial man may be a logician, but he is still mainly an irrational and unconscious being with a strong need to develop his insight and wisdom.

Let us look at some contexts where simple cause-and-effect thinking in today's world often goes wrong: Aid in too many contexts leads to worse conditions and more helplessness. Rapid industrialization of the developing countries too often leaves them worse off. Price reduction to beat competitors may, as exemplified earlier, lead to your own fall. Medical help curing early stress symptoms may open the way for a lethal heart attack later on for a busy business executive. Paying your employees higher wages may lead to decreased performance in a longer time perspective.

An international management consulting company has gone into the red. The company's senior management exerted strong pressure on country managers and key personnel to rectify the condition. Increased sales was the only point of focus. Detailed follow-up of sales prospects was started and international management representatives began to travel and hold sales seminars and motivation sessions. Country managers were instructed to speed up invoicing and give more sales targets for all major clients.

But the results of these "sensible" activities were unexpected: Client managers and other senior personnel left the company, the majority went to competitors. This further affected the results in a negative direction. Again, the management tried a "sensible" action: The company raised prices by an average of 15% to compensate for lost clients and prospects. But this led to even greater loss of customers. The result of these "sensible" actions was a crisis situation where the company tried to find solvent purchasers among its larger competitors.

Let us take as our starting point here a simple, problem-solving strategy. As a formal method it would look like this:

Model for archaic problem solving:

1. Goal.
2. Find the method to reach goal.
3. Decision.

If this is our archaic pattern, we can build on it further: The goal always represents a punctuation. It is a goal, or an end, in a hierarchy of means and ends. It is necessary to check with the goals/ends higher up.

To find means to reach the goal(s), we need to know the status quo. We need an overview of available resources for problem solving and relevant historical data. However, analysis of the present state, its resources, and history should not be elaborated on more than what is relevant for our goal for the problem solving. Generally, too much detail is analyzed in business and industry during problem solving, at the cost of overview and creativity.

The primitive pattern allows for only one solution, the method to reach the goal that instinctively appears. A more advanced pattern should include choice. Even more advanced, it should include the creative making up of new solutions. This should, then, develop our point 2 above into a brainstorming session. Note that brainstorming involves one core aspect of a 3rd order change-process. It also represents a simple understanding at least of hierarchies of means and ends, each end always having more than one means leading toward it.

Having created more than one alternative, we need to sort and evaluate the alternatives with respect to the formulated goal and the governing goals. This, then, should lead us to a first conclusion, a preconclusion. All too often this is identical with the final decision. But something very important is missing. There is a danger that, all along, the problem-solving process has been done in a first position state of thinking. The decision may be okay for me. It may look very smart from my point of view. The advanced thinker, however, will make an appraisal before reaching any conclusion.

This appraisal of the preconclusion should cover: First position, are both the short-term and long-term consequences alright for me/us? Second position, brief and long-term consequences for the other involved, are they alright? Will our decision lead to any form of counteraction? Third position, what are the consequences for the larger system in a short-term and long-term perspective. The appraisal should also draw on the axioms on organizations and archaic man.

The appraisal of the preconclusion may also be seen as a case of feed-forward. Instead of awaiting consequences, we represent them ahead of time, and evaluate them. However obvious this may sound, examples of businesses that overlook this are endless and sometimes rather amusing. An example is Ford exporting its model "Fiera" to Spanish-speaking countries, overlooking the word's Spanish meaning of "ugly old woman," a name that does not promote sales.[2]

The last factor to be mentioned in this connection is fourth position, the analyzing of one's own biases and premises in the above-mentioned three positions.

Now, as advanced thinkers, we can move on to the definite decision, specifying its content, its who, what, where, when, and in which way; and of course, methods for evaluation and further learning by experience. The complete problem-solving strategy now looks like this:

Model for 3rd order problem solving:

1. Goal. The immediate goal and its relation to hierarchies of goals.
2. Present situation. Available resources, limitations, relevant history.
3. Brainstorming. Creative finding of multiple solutions.
4. Sorting and evaluation. Sorting, evaluating and, preconcluding the best alternative(s) leading to the goal.
5. Preconclusion appraisal. First, second, and third position consequences short-term and long-term.
   Evaluation on higher system levels.
   Evaluation of ecosystem patterns and characteristics of ancient man.
   Fourth position evaluation.
6. Decision. Detailing decision and securing evaluation and learning.

The model for 3rd order problem solving then comprises these six frames in the order given. It works as a cognitive pattern of thinking in one man's head only, and, it may serve as a pattern for a group of people being led through a decision-making process. The person leading the process has the responsibility of keeping to the frames, and for going through them in the correct order. In addition to these six frames, we have four secondary frames of use in a 3rd order process.

Summary. It is natural to close each item on the agenda with a summary. Experienced chairmen often do this before moving on to a new item. The summing-up of conclusions is especially important. It is sometimes helpful to summarize the purpose, and the progression, of the meeting.

"As if." This is a secondary frame that is used if the process gets bogged down or otherwise stagnates. The "as if" frame says: "Let us consider that everything is possible . . . that we have unlimited resources . . . that everything is allowed . . . what ideas do we *now* have"? Considerations of reality can, for instance, easily quench signs of creativity. The "as if" frame can be especially helpful as a starting point in item 3 in the described process.

Agreement. Each item will end up with the establishment of an agreement frame, whether expressed or not. The frame is used to finalize items and to allow us to proceed in an atmosphere of cooperation. The summary lays the foundation for the agreement frame.

Agreeing to differ constitutes a special case. Disagreements are often irrelevant, or of lesser importance in relation to problem solving. One special way to use the agreement frame is: "Well, it looks as if we shall have to agree to differ on that particular point . . . let's put it to the side . . . and continue with the job of finding a solution to the real point at issue."

Overview. The procedure is halted temporarily. The person leading the proceedings appraises the entirety of the process, usually in conjunction with the participants. Is it working? Do we need to make some changes to make it work better? This is viewing the process from outside and adjusting in accordance with the actual conditions. It is viewing the entirety rather than the individual parts.

Axiom II.4: Problem Solving

Humans, by evolution, are adapted to environments favoring the taking of actions based on direct, perceivable information and simple cause-and-effect thinking. Modern environments require new problem-solving strategies that have to be learned.
Problem solving considering all mental positions, higher system levels, ecosystem patterns, and characteristics of ancient man should be applied in organizations.

So far so good, since we seem to have progressed from man the hunter to civilized man and his necessarily more complex strategies of problem solving. Good solutions, however, rely not only on good cognitive strategies. The fourth position needs insight. But to exercise insight humans must have some emotional surplus. Few men are in a mental position to exercise advanced insight when fleeing a burning building or in a situation of hot territorial or hierarchical strife. The fourth position needs serenity and a harmonious environment, and a good decision needs good ethics on the part of the decision maker. A useful fourth position also needs some honest insight on the part of the wise problem solver. He should more than know himself. He should understand his irrationality and his biases which originate in personal "unfinished business." And not least, he should be big enough to see this, admit it, and take the consequences of it in his decisions.

Nothing of this comes freely. Our culturally developed environment takes culturally developed personal training, maturity, and, not the least, honesty. A business executive who follows the ecological path should demand this of himself: A learning attitude, high ethics, serenity, and personal honesty.

CHECK YOUR COMPANY: PROBLEM SOLVING

- Are efficient models for problem solving being applied in the organization?
- Are all mental positions regarded in decision making?
- Are representatives for different punctuations and positions invited to state their opinions in decision making?

- Are higher system levels considered in decision making?
- Are patterns of human systems considered?
- Are human territoriality and hierarchies considered?

CHECK YOURSELF: PROBLEM SOLVING

- Apply the questions above to yourself.
- How easily do you perceive your own personal biases and unfinished business?
- Do others perceive you as a person holding a learning attitude, high ethics, and personal honesty?

Part IV

Organizational Ecology and Strategic Leadership

An organization's basic philosophy is more important to its end results than technological and/or economic resources, organizational structure, innovation and choice of time.

Thomas Watson, Jr., in Tad Tuleja, *Beyond the Bottom Line*
[author's translation]

Chapter 16

Strategy: Formality or Reality

> The more limited the interests are formulated in time and space, the
> more one is bound to find the interests "conflicting." The whole world
> over a time span of a thousand years has but common interests.
>
> Anonymous

Today both strategy and leadership are a matter of course. Why is it then,
that so very few enterprises actually practice strategic leadership in *reality*?
That is to say, that strategic plans are formulated, a minimum of ownership
processes are arranged at lower levels, and reporting structures for the
goals are established and used.

Strategy exists most places as a *formality*—something is written about
goals and objectives, somewhere. But few enterprises stand the simplest
check of all: the questioning of middle managers and other employees to
state the elements of the strategy. What are the strategic goals, what are
the strategic focus areas, what are the values and ethical guidelines of the
enterprise? In surveys conducted to map this, even well-reputed corporations score down to zero on a scale from zero to one hundred! Below
top management, ignorance often rules. Enthusiastic cooperation throughout the organization for unknown goals, according to unknown guidelines,
is not very probable! Attractive brochures and posters are then often
shown to be of little value. Strategy as reality implies real organizational
consensus on the core elements of the strategy in question.

The reasons for lack of real strategic leadership can be many. Some top
managers want to keep all roads open, without being bound to follow
previously decided paths. They want to maintain flexibility. Sometimes

they have hidden agendas that would surface if the strategy were to be overtly formulated. In some cases the middle management tries to avoid strategy and leadership because it wants to be free to side with the top one day, and with the bottom the next day—even on the same topic. Many managers perceive overt and unequivocal leadership as threatening. If they stick their neck out it might be cut off. Strategic decisions are also sometimes unpopular, not least in times with lay-offs. Also, when practicing strategic leadership, a manager's incompetence as a leader might well become evident.

Sometimes processes like those to be presented in this part of the book are avoided simply because they take time. Time costs money. There are so many good reasons—and many of them are even respectable and sensible.

No strategy and no leadership may be alright on a dreamy pacific island. But in an environment with ever-faster changing technology, markets and international politics, and with ever-stronger competition, long-term survival depends on strategy and leadership. The competitive enterprises of today and tomorrow must be lean, delayered, decentralized, flexible and must practice delegation. Such enterprises need a strategy, and this strategy must be known, owned, and practiced by all hands. Leadership must be practiced at all management levels.

THE STRUCTURE OF A STRATEGIC PLAN

An organization must first of all have an identity—a *business description*, as I call it here. Then it should formulate its general purpose, make a *mission statement*. It should have a *vision* for its activities, it must know where it's going. It needs *main goals* which lead onward toward the vision, and are in accordance with the vision. It should have an *action plan* containing the objectives and actions needed to achieve the main goals. Its *policy*, or *ethical guidelines*, should be formulated and should characterize its practice. Finally: The management teams should agree on a *common management philosophy* (see also Appendix 3). All this comprises what I choose to call the organization's *strategy document* (Figure 16.1).

The organization should formulate its strategy at the levels relevant for its size and complexity. For larger corporations, one usually talks of corporate level strategy (or top-level strategy), SBU (Strategic Business Unit), or business level and functional level.

As a rule of thumb, all elements of the strategy document should be formulated at corporate level. Objectives and action plans will then only be formulated for special strategic projects and reported directly to the corporate management. The formulations at the corporate level will set the frameworks and directions for the lower levels.

At SBU level, mission statements and policy and ethical guidelines from

Figure 16.1
The Structure of a Business Strategy at Corporate Level and SBU Level

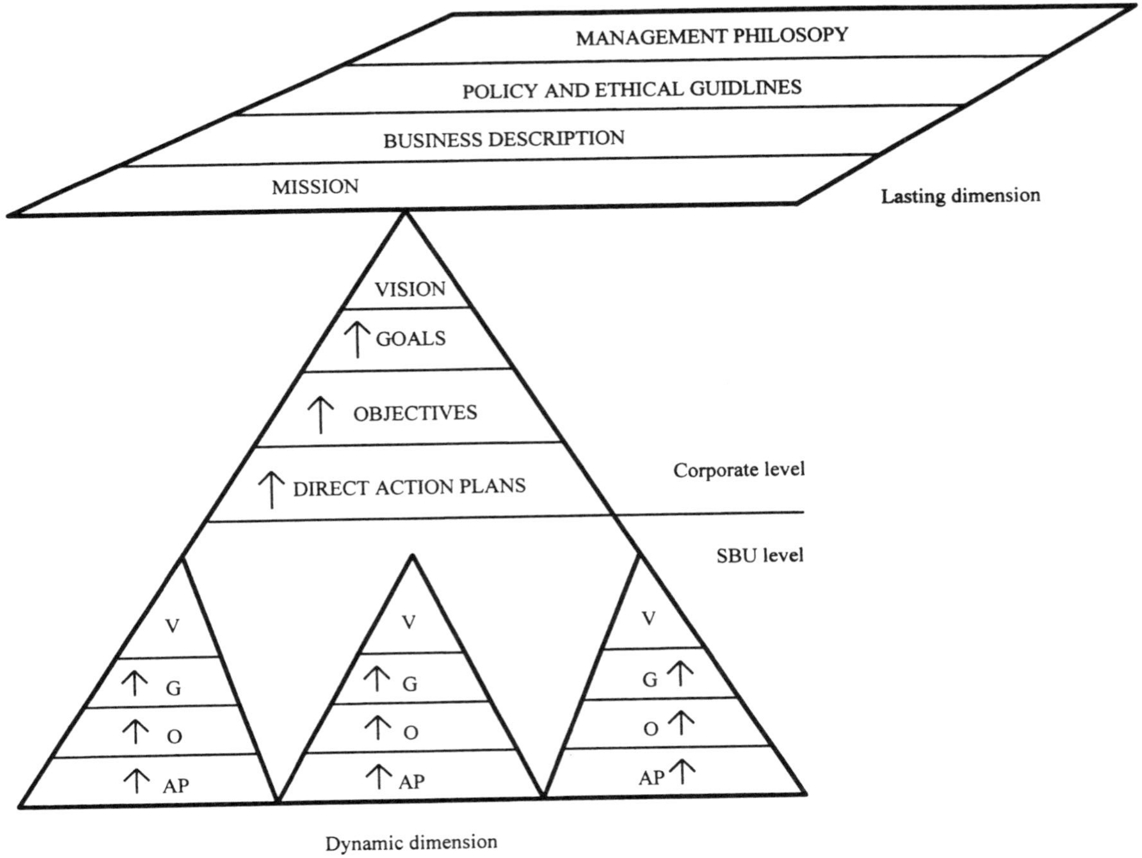
MANAGEMENT PHILOSOPY
POLICY AND ETHICAL GUIDLINES
BUSINESS DESCRIPTION
MISSION
Lasting dimension
VISION
GOALS
OBJECTIVES
DIRECT ACTION PLANS
Corporate level
SBU level
V
G
O
AP
V
G
O
AP
V
G
O
AP
Dynamic dimension

corporate level mainly stand unchanged. This also often applies to management philosophy. The other elements are usually formulated also at SBU level. And again, objectives and action plans are formulated for special strategic projects, with reporting to SBU top management. Beside this, the further detailing of objectives and actions leading to the SBU main goals and vision is delegated to functional level.

The frameworks for the strategy formulations at functional level are set by the superior levels. At functional level, usually only objectives and action plans are developed.

Three viewpoints of importance should be mentioned: First, *the strategy document should not cover all activities.* Everyday activities should rely on the employees' responsible decisions and the management's ability to practice unbureaucratic leadership. Organizations with plans covering all activities will be rigid and lose vitality. The goals, objectives, and action plans should not cover the total activity. A strategy document covering "everything" is like a communist five-year plan, reducing managers to bureaucrats who control labor. Space must be left open for managerial initiatives and responsibilities, for self-organizing, for strategic leadership.

Second, *the strategy document has no value in and by itself.* A piece of paper has no value, it is the processes of development and ownership and the final implementation that count. The purpose of strategic planning is change, and the development of the thinking and practice of all hands in a common direction—the strategic direction. The strategy document is a means, not an end. It makes the strategic direction and priorities visible. And, as Kotter and Heskett have shown, changes are made more easily with the visible than the invisible in an organizational culture.[1]

Third, *no strategic plan remains good forever.* Any plan involves a danger of rigidity. At the point in time when a plan is made, certain factors are known. But today the environment and information change so quickly that revisions and rethinking should be regarded as a continuous process, and not limited to the yearly or half-yearly strategy meeting.

APPLYING 3RD ORDER PROCESSES FOR DEVELOPING A STRATEGIC PLAN

In theory, 3rd order principles for change and leadership could mean "everyone taking part in everything": This would give maximum identification with the strategic plan at all levels and thereby, again in theory, the best basis for work. But this can really only be done in one-man operations. The ideal should be an *optimum* degree of openness and participation, as well as the identification of the best process for strategy development, and ownership, as the following example will illustrate.

The R&D department of a European corporation went through a comprehensive program for organizational development. The management was very democratic minded and strove to get the employees involved in a strategy development process. The consultants responsible for the organizational development program were given a relatively free hand in guiding the process the first time it was attempted. At one time, as many as 200 employees out of a total of 300 participated in groups associated with the process.

The conflict potential rose to an alarming level both within and between groups. Production levels reached their nadir, and there came a point when the management realized the seriousness of the situation and demanded a drastic tightening-up of the activity. It took another three months before the department had completed the process and was back to normal; the after-effects of "the process period," as it was referred to later, were felt for a long time.

In large organizations, different groups need to be represented and informed. But all decisions cannot be discussed at all levels. Successful companies may go a long way in involving all levels of the organization in the comprehensive strategy development. At the same time, a strictly limited and guided process is essential.

The model for 3rd order strategy development shown here must be adapted to suit the individual organization's type, size, and management. At the same time, it has proven effective in organizations of very different types and in different cultures. It represents a seemingly well-balanced compromise between open, 3rd order processes across levels on the one hand, and strict frameworks for the processes, and respect for the organizational hierarchy, on the other.

Model for 3rd order strategy development:

1. *Business description and vision.* Top management, possibly in cooperation with the board of directors, shapes the organization's business description and vision by means of a 3rd order problem-solving process. Before a final conclusion, the preconcluded formulations are checked with representatives from the second and third positions. If a business description and vision that is up-to-date and of high quality already exists, this point represents just a minor freshing up.

2. *Strategic main goals.* The top management develops and works toward a strong consensus on the strategic main goals for the strategy period under discussion. Based on a SWOT analysis (internal Strengths and Weaknesses, external Opportunities and Threats) and information of future scenarios, the work takes the form of a 3rd order process within the top management. The preconcluded main goals are checked with representatives from the second and third positions before a final conclusion is made. The business description, vision, and main goals are "sold" and firmly entrenched at middle-management level. Middle-management then "sells" the business description and vision further down in the lower echelons of the organization.

3. *Strategic objectives and plans of action.* The top and middle management, in cooperation, establish working groups across departmental or divisional lines,

and across levels. Some groups also include representatives from customers and/ or suppliers. The working groups' terms of reference are to generate suggestions for objectives, and for activities in accordance with these objectives. Usually each group works on one single, strategic goal. Representatives from the working groups present the group's suggestions to the top management, which accepts or rejects the various proposals. The top management itself takes on the duty of thoroughly explaining any rejections.

4. *The complete strategy document.* The final strategy document is determined at top management level, before being "sold" internally, first to supervisors and thereafter by supervisors to employees at all levels.

The process described here represents a combined top-down and bottom-up procedure. (The process does not include mission, policy, and ethical guidelines and management philosophy. These elements will usually be of a more lasting nature. There are examples of mission statements that remain unchanged for more than a hundred years!) The mission statement and policy and ethical guidelines should also definitely be known and owned by all employees, whereas the management philosophy should be seen as a living reference for management decisions and practice.

Let us look at an example of a very comprehensive process of strategy development and ownership, which goes on for a little more than three months. The organization is a national corporation with approximately 10,000 employees divided between a central staff and six district branch offices. A corporate-level strategy document has already been formulated by the central staff, in cooperation with the district branch directors. This contains, at a corporate level, business description, vision, mission statement, policy and ethical guidelines, and management philosophy. What was to be obtained now was strategic goals, objectives, and action plans at branch level. The following schedule was formulated and followed.

01. Project week 01:
The branch management, together with a representative from another branch, is to hold a two-day seminar to establish the branch's main goals for the coming strategy period. Preliminary work covers an extensive SWOT analysis. Scenarios are formulated and distributed to the branch management by the central staff. The branch managers also shall establish strategy working groups for each main goal.
02. Project week 02:
The strategy working groups are to commence work in two weeks. The groups comprise people from different areas in the district, together with a "guest" from another branch office.
03. Project week 04:
The strategy groups are to present their results to the branch management.
04. Project week 05:
The branch departments are to work on and refine the material from the strategy groups at a seminar for the branch management.

05. Project week 06:
Distribution of the first draft of a strategy document for each branch to all six branch management teams and to the central staff.
06. Project week 07:
Feedback to the individual branch director on his local strategy document from the central staff and the other branch directors.
07. Project week 08:
Issue in the branch organization of the revised first draft of the strategy document for the branch. Invitation to all employees to comment.
08. Project week 10:
Comments from employees to be evaluated at a branch management meeting. Final revision of branch strategy document.
09. Project week 12:
Central staff and branch directors to evaluate the sum of branch strategy documents and compare them with corporate strategic goals. Plan to be agreed for internal marketing of strategy in all branches.
10. Project week 13:
Issuing of the final branch strategy document, also containing corporate-level business description, vision, mission statement, policy and ethical guidelines, and strategic goals, in each branch organization respectively. Branch strategy containing goals, objectives, and action plans for each branch, respectively.

3rd order strategy development will often result in the development of a large number of detailed documents per division, department, group, and so on. Involvement of the lower echelons in the organization has many positive aspects. But as the example from the R&D department showed, it is important to have clear and concise guidelines for processes such as these. The following is an example of instructions to a strategy group.

Instruction to strategy group 1:
The aim of the group is to produce a proposal for an activity plan in order to achieve goal A. The proposal for the activity plan should contain a description of activities, time schedule with deadlines, proposal for subobjectives or milestones, and proposals for participants/person(s) responsible for the activities. The proposal is expected to have a broad basis among the department employees. It is not expected to be qualitatively cut and polished. At all events, the proposal should be refined further by the department manager. The group is expected to work in a flexible manner and within a tight time frame in order to disturb the normal running of the company as little as possible.

Meeting 1. Time frame 2 hours:

1. Establishment of the group. Establishment of leadership of the group.

2. Establishment of a common understanding of goal A.

3. Distribution of the department's employees among the group participants (who talks with whom).

4. Practical details.

5. Initial brainstorming on possible activities related to goal A.

Task prior to meeting 2: Collect ideas for activities from the department employees.

Meeting 2. Time frame 3 hours:

1. Collection of incoming ideas for activities.

2. Second brainstorming on activities related goal A.

3. Initial rough sorting of the proposed activities.

4. Practical details.

Task prior to meeting 3: Collect comments on the roughly sorted activities from the department's employees.

Meeting 3. Time frame 3 hours:

1. Discussion of the roughly sorted activities together with collected comments.

2. Sorting and evaluation of activities.

3. Rough formulation of activity plan.

Task prior to presentation (group leader only): Prepare presentation of activity plan. Group leader presents the results to the department management.

3rd order strategy development is a powerful activity for obtaining unity from top to bottom in the organization. At the same time, as mentioned in the opening section, there is a danger of wasting time and of becoming bureaucratic. 3rd order processes should always be combined with clear-cut goals, time schedules, and responsibilities.

LINKING ORGANIZATIONAL ECOLOGY WITH STRATEGIC LEADERSHIP

Our concepts of strategic leadership and organizational ecology should conform with many of today's dominating trends in management thinking: Decentralization of power, empowering of lower ranks, project and network organization, management by delegation, delayering, fractal organization, and human resources valuation.

How are strategic leadership and organizational ecology connected? Let us progress in consecutive order according to our preceding axioms:

I.1: Common Interests

Whenever destructive conflicts arise, the main reason is that the involved "parties" are not aware that they are parts of a system on which they all depend. In such situations there is usually a lack of common goals. Strategy contains the common goals, identity, and ethics. Without strategy, the organization easily becomes fragmented into departments, professional groups, and working groups, without cooperation or synergy. Hence, strategic leadership prevents destructive conflicts, and also provides a solid basis as a common point of reference when conflicts are to be solved.

I.2: Self-Organizing

The company and its parts are complex, self-organizing, and self-correcting systems. Delegation, empowering, and decentralization of power provide the best opportunities for sound self-organizing. The people who live daily with the challenges are also the specialists to solve them. 3rd order strategy development is in accordance with this principle.

I.3: Theoretical Optimums

The processes also give the best of opportunities to ensure the formulation of optimum levels for goals and objectives. This is because all levels and all lines participate actively. Chances are also high that the company will stick to the optimum goals, since these goals are "owned" by all groups.

I.4: Feedback

Any breach in internal or external feedback loops is a threat to the company. Feedback should be encouraged, and should be regarded as a matter of course, and also an obvious duty of any employee. Feedback is encouraged and placed in system in 3rd order strategy development processes and in the implementation procedures. 3rd order strategy development processes represent an opening up of the system, for extensive flow of information and opinions. At the same time, the flow is controlled, channelled, and in accordance with the hierarchy. External representatives also are invited to participate, on a controlled basis. This represents a balance of "not too open, not too closed." A strategy that is owned by all hands ensures identity and focus.

I.5: Diversity

Strategic leadership in general, and the processes mentioned especially, make decisions and actions visible and unequivocal. This gives room for open discussion and diversity of opinions. The organizational diversity is exploited in the 3rd order strategy development processes, since groups are set up with representatives from all lines and levels.

I.6: Conditions for Results

Ongoing 3rd order processes should be strictly led, and should follow certain patterns. Unless this is taken seriously, the situation could take a turn for the worse. The result could be power struggles, bureaucracy, demotivation, and wasted time. The context, syntax, and the developmental stage of the system must be considered. Moreover, the comprehensive strategy processes, as described above, establish the necessary common points of reference. One of the strengths of the 3rd order strategy development process lies in the directness of communication across all levels through the group work.

The 3rd order strategy development process represents a minor investment of man-hours. It really represents a low-energy influence of high-energy effect, since it is directed at the core of the organization. 3rd order processes and strategic leadership in general also are energy-saving, contrary to what many managers seem to believe. No single factor steals more from organizational productivity than unspoken disagreements, the hidden building of alliances, and covert corporate "politics!"

I.7: Function Replacement

Open contact across levels, and the inclusion of second and third position representatives in impact analysis, help to map the consequences of upcoming actions. This provides the best of opportunities to substitute existing functions.

II.1: Territoriality

Without strategy, no common territory is defined. Then individuals and groups define their own territory, which is defended and given superiority, even over the interests of the company. Motivation to perform for the company diminishes, motivation to fight for one's own interests or those of one's own group (against others in the company) increases. Strategic leadership and 3rd order management processes prevent this state of affairs.

The 3rd order strategy development process helps to establish contributions to governing common goals as the dominant factor of motivation. Also, the existence of commonly owned strategic goals provides the best of opportunities for establishing reward systems that are linked to strategic performance, and are perceived as fair.

The "we-feeling" is directly enforced through 3rd order leadership processes. The processes also serve as models for constructive behavior, communication, and decision making.

II.2: Hierarchies

Without clear leadership, a lasting struggle to establish the missing hierarchy starts off. This is often wrongly understood as an expression of man's need of power. But this struggle is most often superfluous. A clear-cut hierarchy based on strategic leadership is the necessary first step to prevent "power struggles." The channelling of disagreements and diversity of opinions through structured 3rd order processes helps to turn the energy of the organization in the right direction.

11.3: Man's Natural Environment

3rd order processes conform with our notion of a healthy mental and social working environment. These processes invite all hands to participate in planning and learning by feedback. They help to provide an understandable picture of the organization and its environment, its course, and development. They turn the organization into a surveyable unit.

II.4: Problem Solving

3rd order processes represent an excellent way of synergetic learning. Intelligent problem solving is learned through practical participation in different groups, and the competence acquired is transferred to other contexts.

The old days of "we do this because the Boss says so" are slowly disappearing in modern enterprises. Overt strategic leadership and 3rd order processes are helping to do away with this state of affairs. The modern strategic leader holds his position as long as he is able to convince his subordinates that he is right, through knowledge, reasoning, and capable leadership.

Strategic leadership and 3rd order management processes find comprehensive theoretical confirmation in organizational ecology, as described so far. Empirical knowledge also strongly supports the necessity of strategic leadership. The studies of successful enterprises in the 1980s and 1990s show that values and strategic goals are deeply rooted in the corporate culture of those enterprises, and that their managers practice more active leadership than mere administrative management.[2]

CHECK YOUR COMPANY: STRATEGY

You can easily check the degree of strategy ownership among middle managers and employees:

- Give a sample of them a questionnaire, where they are asked to fill in the company's vision, mission, goals, and objectives for the present strategy period (without looking it up).
- Ask a sample of them for the outcome of different activities they are busy with. Check whether the outcomes given are in accordance with the strategy.
- Apply all questions from Chapter 5 on common interests and conflict solving.
- Are the different elements of the strategy referred to as points of reference whenever decisions are made in the company?
- Does the strategy document meet the criteria for being well formed (see Appendix 3)?

CHECK YOURSELF: STRATEGY

- Is the company's strategy your point of reference in your decision making?
- Do you apply strategic thinking in your own professional life?

Chapter 17

Implementation, Flexibility, and Resistance

I received a letter from my daughter-in-law last week in which she told me about her daughter's sixth birthday. The next day she did something for which her mother reprimanded her, and she told her mother: "It's awfully hard to be six years old. I've only had one day's experience."

Milton H. Erickson, in Sidney Rosen, *My Voice Will Go with You*

The managerial challenges to the practitioners of strategic leadership surface when it comes to implementation. Planning and talking are easy, managing the development and ownership processes is more challenging. But the most difficult is to put it all into practice—to get the job done. However, without high-quality implementation, the process would have been better not done. Disappointment and demotivation in an organization which faces its own inability to implement plans are very serious setbacks.

Let us look at a few basic preconditions for successful implementation of the strategy.

Overview of activities conditional for strategy implementation:

1. Quantifying of all goals and objectives.
2. Reporting of progress.
3. Information and feedback to all levels.
4. Adjustment of the strategy.

Strategic goals and objectives must be *quantified*. A formulation like "opening new markets as soon as possible" is an example of an unquantified strategic goal. The criteria for whether it is reached or not are unclear. "Opening three new markets in the former East European countries within two years and with gross sales of at least $8 million in each country" is an example of a well-quantified goal. A manager, both for his own planning and for reporting purposes, needs formulations like the last one. They give him a sound basis for reporting; will the goal be reached? Some time ahead he then knows whether extra action is necessary.

Can all goals and objectives be quantified? With few exceptions, the answer is "yes." Possible exceptions are typical qualitative objectives, such as "developing and implementing a new organizational structure within six months." The question "has the objective been reached" might easily be answered with a "yes" or "no," instead of with a quantitative statement.

What about objectives like "improved psychosocial working climate?" Can this be quantified? Yes, either by direct measurement, for example, through a questionnaire survey to employees. Or, if this is not feasible, a regular hearing among the managers and a sample of their subjective judgements may suffice. A third possibility is to ask: "How will a change in psychosocial working climate become evident?" Common answers could be: number of days absent through (work-related) illness, and levels of productivity. Changes in these parameters then can be taken as indications of changes in the psychosocial working climate.

When the parameter is chosen, a baseline must be established first. This will usually take time, so that the quantification of many goals and objectives often has to take place some time after the general planning session and the strategy developmental processes have been completed.

The reporting of strategic progress is twofold. It contains a written part, showing whether the planned actions have been implemented in practice and whether the parameters show the planned progress. The other part of the reporting is oral, and should take place at regular strategic management meetings. The frequency of such strategic meetings depends on the organizational level (usually more frequent meetings at lower levels), and on the properties of the goals and objectives. The strategic management meetings also function as fora for information and feedback.

Information and feedback: The sound enterprise should practice information policies according to the axioms of organizational ecology. The most important principle to be followed is that everybody should be honestly informed about the company's failures or successes. This provides a strengthening of the common territory, the "we" feeling. It also provides feedback, which was described as a precondition for motivation and meaning. To give a brief example: In a company in recession, the CEO heavily reprimanded the market department for passivity. He had forgotten, however, to check second position, the market department. It turned out that they had not been informed of the serious situation, and therefore lacked the motivation for extraordinary effort!

The world has thoroughly learned this principle through experiences from the former Soviet Union and other communist societies. There is no doubt that their general retention and twisting of information contributed to their fall. But the idea of filtering information for tactical purposes is still all too popular in many business enterprises.

The opening of information flows in and out of the organization is another characteristic of the sound enterprise. Closeness to customers and the market presupposes open information. Benchmarking procedures and audits will become more common; they both imply openness.

The growth in the quantity of information poses a special challenge. Information seems to grow exponentially. The more details and facts that are processed, the more difficult it is to keep the overall picture clear. Strict limitations on information and standards for brevity will become ever more important. Done with a respectful hand this should improve a psychosocial climate, not threaten it.

The transformation of information into electronic signals presents yet another challenge. I believe that the enterprises that stick, whenever possible, to face-to-face discussions and information, and do not substitute these with exchange of opinions or news on the data network, will gain a competitive advantage by so doing. Face-to-face contact has qualities that cannot be passed on through electronic devices. These qualities cover interhuman contact, nonverbal signalling, social communication and immediate adjustment of messages, and clearing up of misunderstandings. Ideally, serious reprimands should never be sent by electronic devices alone! The same goes for important brainstorming sessions.

In old-fashioned organizations distinguished by 1st order management style, reporting and information go only from the bottom and up, while feedback goes only from the top and down. Not so in modern environments distinguished by 3rd order managerial processes. Information on strategic progress definitely should reach all levels, and managerial open-mindedness should allow for mutual feedback. Especially in organizations that have established good strategic ownership processes, more democratic information and feedback routines are a must.

However, it is essential to think in terms of optimum, not maximum. The potential amount of information is enormous, if one believes that "everybody should know as much as possible." The essential information needed at the lower levels is the information that provides a basis for answering these questions: How is the company, "we," doing? What is the contribution I and my group should make? Has our performance been satisfactory according to our strategic vision, goals, and objectives? Should we make adjustments to our work?

The strategic management meetings also constitute the framework for strategic *adjustments*. Changes in the environment, and information from the strategic reporting, may give reason for adjustments. Solid planning and ownership processes should not prevent flexible and open-minded adjustments of the strategic plans when there is good reason for such! If it does, then strategic leadership has turned into a bureaucratic device, not an aid for successful business.

In any situation of strategy implementation, or implementation of changes in general, one may meet the phenomenon of *resistance to change*. The common manager has a tendency to conceive resistance as unwillingness, lack of motivation, incompetence, ignorance, or even indolence or sabotage. But usually this first position reaction misses the point—and creates deadlocks rather than opportunities. From the perspective of third position, and applying the concepts of organizational ecology, a whole lot of hypotheses on the situation can be generated, leading to concrete action.

Resistance checklist:

1. Unsound changes. When resistance to change occurs, it is necessary to check a very simple first hypothesis, namely: Maybe the "resisters" are right, and I am wrong! Maybe my employees or middle managers know something that I as a top manager do not know, and the resistance is a feedback to me, saying: "Check once more, from second and third position, the consequences of your planned actions. Make the necessary adjustments, and the resistance will disappear." To state it differently:
   Hypothesis: The changes are unsound for the company.
   Action: Revise and adjust changes.

2. Misunderstandings. A next, very simple hypothesis generated from the second position perspective is: Maybe the resistance is there because of misunderstandings and misinterpretations. If this is the case, you need to check how the plans are understood and clear up the misunderstandings, and then the resistance will disappear:
   Hypothesis: The changes are misunderstood or misinterpreted.
   Action: Explain changes.

3. Missing information. Resistance also occurs when the larger perspective or the connection with the strategic goals are unknown to the employees:
   Hypothesis: The changes are perceived as meaningless or out of connection with the main strategy.
   Action: Inform about the strategy and the connection between this and the changes. Explain larger perspective.

4. Wrong process. When processes are applied that are out of tune with the competence level and the organizational culture, resistance may occur:
   Hypothesis: The process of change chosen is out of tune.
   Action: Adjust and apply other processes of change.

5. Common interests. Referring to our axioms of organizational ecology, a hand-

ful of hypotheses and opportunities for sound action to prevent or overcome resistance emerge:

Hypothesis: The changes are out of tune with the overall strategy.
Action: Revise and adjust changes.

6. Self-organizing.
Hypothesis: The changes are planned or implemented in a way that unnecessarily removes authority from employees, and/or degrades the employees to mere executers of readily made decisions.
Action: Engage employees in the planning of the changes/delegate more authority to implement.

7. Optimum levels.
Hypothesis: The goals are formulated with "as much/as little as possible" measures, and therefore perceived as unhealthy or frustrating to the employees.
Action: Correct the formulations to "optimum" and quantified formulations.

8. Feedback and openness.
Hypothesis: The objectives and plans for changes are made in the top management's closed room.
Action: Open the system to information from lower levels, customers, and the environment in general.

9. Diversity.
Hypothesis: The changes threaten the diversity of the organization.
Action: Revise and adjust changes.

10. Conditions for results.
Hypothesis: The changes imply burdensome work for little gain, are wrongly timed; actions appear in wrong order; are bureaucratic; are out of tune with the stage of development of the system.
Action: Revise and adjust changes.

11. Function replacement.
Hypothesis: The changes imply lost functions or responsibilities for "the resisters," without giving any substitutes.
Action: Find function replacements based on a win-win attitude.

12. Territoriality.
Hypothesis: The changes are perceived as a threat to someone's territory.
Action: Define a common territory. Find tasks for common effort. Arrange for 3rd order processes for common goals and objectives.

13. Hierarchies.
Hypothesis: The changes are introduced in a manner that is not in accordance with the hierarchy, leading to resistance from those who find themselves bypassed.
Action: Revise the plans and reestablish the hierarchy.

14. Working environments.
Hypothesis: The changes imply a degradation of the physical, psychological, or social working environment.

Actions: Revise and adjust changes.

15. Problem-solving.
Hypothesis: The changes are decided on a simple cause-and-effect basis.
Action: Revise and apply the 3rd order problem-solving model.

In organizational ecological theory the hypothesis of laziness or ignorance on the part of "the resisters" to change is the last in the row. Or, to put it briefly: (1) There is no such thing as indolent co-workers; "indolence" is created by incompetent managers; (2) There is no such thing as resistance; what looks like resistance really is feedback: "You are doing the wrong thing—do something else."

CHECK YOUR COMPANY: IMPLEMENTATION

- How often are plans made and then not implemented?
- How often are plans implemented, and the objectives not achieved?
- Are objectives quantified when plans are decided?
- Are information and feedback as often as possible passed on in face-to-face settings, rather than as written material?
- Is information about progress reaching both the persons responsible and the persons implementing the plans?
- How easily are plans revised and adjusted?
- To which extent is resistance a problem in the company?

CHECK YOURSELF: IMPLEMENTATION

- Apply the questions above to yourself.

Chapter 18

3rd Order Processes in Organizations

> If he is truly wise, he will not invite you to enter his house of wisdom,
> but lead you instead to the threshold of your own wisdom.
> Kahlil Gibran, *The Prophet* [author's translation]

Organizations in an educated and complex world need employees that can analyze and decide independently. Management, by the very nature of its management style, can promote or prevent independence, responsibility, and creativity among employees. All management implies communication. Let us look at communication in accordance with the principles of the 1st, 2nd, and 3rd order processes described earlier. We can divide communication into categories, as in our treatment of the processes of change. We then get the following overview.

Overview of three categories of communication:

1st order communication: The communication is such that the recipient carries out actions without appraising alternatives.

2nd order communication: The communication is such that the recipient appraises the given alternatives, and selects the best.

3rd order communication: The communication is such that the recipient develops alternatives himself, appraises them, and chooses among them.

Example of 1st order communication: Message from CEO to marketing director: "Start the marketing of product A on Thursday of next week, in accordance with the instructions I have worked out and laid on your desk."

Example of 2nd order communication: Message from CEO to marketing director: "Consider which of the proposed elements for a plan for the marketing of product A we should choose, and come back for a discussion and decision on the matter on Friday."

Example of 3rd order communication: Message from CEO to marketing director: "Based on this year's company strategy, will you kindly propose activities for product A, placing emphasis on the future marketing situation? Please advise when you feel ready to discuss the matter."

The opportunities for 3rd order communication develop over time. An employee who is new to the job must often be guided by someone acquainted with the system. As he gradually becomes familiar with the work routines, the employee can make some decisions within given guidelines. After a further "running in" period, and having acquired knowledge of the whole process, company priorities, and culture, most people are able to handle 3rd order communication.

We can also superimpose the three categories of change-processes on management processes in general. We then talk of 1st, 2nd, and 3rd order management styles. Some employees and managers never reach the necessary level of independence and responsibility so that they can be led by principles of 3rd order management. They have to be guided and supervised in detail, even after several years in the company. It can be useful for managers occasionally to take stock in this area: Which of my junior managers/employees are capable of handling 3rd order management? Who responds positively to 1st order and who handles 2nd order? As a rule for communication in management we can say: *The messages must lie within the recipient's capacity for delegation (responsibility, authority, independence) and at the same time be as close to 3rd order management as he is personally capable of.* In this way the recipient of messages and tasks will be met at his own level of competence, while at the same time developing independence and a sense of responsibility (Figure 18.1).

There is no doubt that 3rd order management is desirable, it is also probably a sheer necessity in an environment of rapid change and amounts of information insurmountable to one single top manager. Delegation is the answer, and 3rd order processes represent the best method. But if 3rd order management style is to operate in a constructive manner, certain conditions *must* be met.

Summary of conditions for 3rd order management:

1. The manager should have the necessary personal competence in handling interpersonal relationships.

2. The level under the manager should have the necessary competence in its specific subject and be able and willing to take on responsibility.

3. The organizational hierarchy should be clear-cut and strong.

Figure 18.1
Development of Your Management Style

Write the names of your subordinates in the column to the left. Fill in the squares where each belongs with respect to his activities in general to be led by 1st, 2nd, or 3rd order management, according to his present competence level. Place a cross in the two squares to the right from the ones you filled in. The two squares with crosses show you a desired and realistic development of your management style with respect to each of your subordinates.

Direction for development →

Name of subordinate	1st order Management			2nd order Management			3rd order Management		
1									
2									
3									
4									
5									
6									
7									

4. The strategy and important priorities should be firmly entrenched within the organization.

5. Reporting and information routines should operate satisfactorily.

3rd order management in surroundings that do not comply with these five conditions easily leads to frustration and conflict, and often also to loss of efficiency and productivity.

3RD ORDER PROCESSES FOR IMPROVEMENT

In the wake of strategy ownership processes, the conditions for improvements are the best. All hands know the strategic direction and the objectives, which gives both motivation and clear frames of relevance.

Let us go through a generic process for applying 3rd order work for improvement. Here I call the object for improvement the "focus area." Note that the focus could be on anything from quality and productivity to ecological environment, or the implementation of new technology. Let us not forget the conditions for 3rd order management mentioned above. The same conditions apply if these processes are to work out satisfactorily.

Model for 3rd order work for improvement:

Precondition: Strategy ownership. The participants should share knowledge and a sense of ownership of the organization's strategy (see the model for 3rd order strategy development).

1. Establishment and ownership of focus area objectives. It is the management within the respective fields who decides the units of measure and the focus area objectives after discussions across levels. External or internal benchmarking are possible aids to this process. The objectives must be accepted and "owned" by the participants in the process.

2. Working groups and preliminary plans. Working groups are professionally schooled in the relevant area. It is ideal that such groups have members from different levels, and also from different lines when relevant to the focus area. They are given guidelines for their work which resemble those for the strategy group's work, mentioned earlier. Each group's mandate is to arrive at actions that might improve the performance in its focus area.

3. Development of final plans. The management within the fields in question appraises the proposals from the working groups. The groups must be told the reason for all rejections of proposals. The management then develops the final plans of action.

4. Preconclusion appraisal. The preconceived results of implementation are then appraised (from the first, second, and third position), generally by the management in question, as well as by the next higher level in the hierarchy. Necessary adjustments to the plans are made.

5. Decision. The management in question, in agreement with next higher level in the hierarchy, makes a final decision to implement the plans.

6. Implementation. The activities are put into effect. This includes both implementation of activities and installation of necessary checks and follow-up routines.

The processes of strategy formulation and ownership very often uncover needs for major reorganization of the company. Unlike other areas, this is an area which rarely invites 3rd order processes. It seems that, even in companies that are strategically led, in a reorganizing situation the tendency for all to stick one-sided to their first position perspective is a major obstacle to a broad and open process across levels. Groups that are given the task of proposing improvements for strategic and productivity reasons may well come up with proposals for reorganizing. From there on, however, I recommend primarily a strict top-down procedure.

CHECK YOUR COMPANY: MANAGEMENT PROCESSES

- Which of the three categories of communication is typical in the company?
- Are all three categories applied on different occasions?
- Which conditions for 3rd order management are most typically not met in the company?
- Does the management philosophy clearly state the desired management style?
- Is there consensus in the management about the desired management style?

CHECK YOURSELF: MANAGEMENT PROCESSES

- Apply the questions above to yourself.
- Are you conscious of which of your co-workers respond positively to the respective categories of management and communication?
- What kind of personal adjustments do you need to make to develop your abilities and flexibility as a 1st, 2nd, and 3rd order manager?
- Do you assist your co-managers in their development of competence in flexible 1st, 2nd, and 3rd order management?

Part V

The Ecological Path

We are learning by bitter experience that the organism which destroys its environment, destroys itself.

Gregory Bateson, *Mind and Nature*

Chapter 19

Ecological Values

> We need types of societies and communities in which one delights in
> the value-creative aspects of equilibrium rather than the glorification
> of value-neutral growth; in which being together with other living be-
> ings is more important than exploiting or killing them.
>
> Arne Naess, *Ecology, Community and Lifestyle*

THE NEED FOR ECOLOGICAL CHANGE

Let us make an experiment of thought: A worldwide expert group has
done extensive research on the state of the biosphere through the last
thirty years. Their conclusions are unanimous:

There is no danger for man, neither to his existence nor his health, because of
continued and unlimited industrial and economic growth all over the planet. Exploitation of raw materials can go on, there are no limits. The same goes for
energy. Pollution is no problem. Even so-called endangered species can adapt or
will be replaced without problems. Mother Earth can handle five billion cars today,
seven billion cars by the turn of the century, ten billion by 2010 and so on. The
same goes for washing machines, refrigerators, television sets, dishwashers, mix-
masters, private planes, helicopters and cabin cruisers. The ozone layer is thick
enough for ever, global warming is a myth, CO_2 is naturally balanced, no matter
the amount of emissions. Even over-population turns out to be no problem. The
earth can sustain fifty billion people through new agricultural technology. Gaya
can develop into a materialistic paradise for everybody beyond limits.

In this situation the conclusion should be clear: Let's go on, and make
a materialistic heaven on earth, with the industrialized nations as loco-

motives, new technology as fuel, the worldwide free market as machinery, and the market mechanisms as a steering unit. Let's do it! There are, however, two complicating factors.

First, economic and materialistic growth is a means, not an end. It is a means to the end "a better life," not the end itself. According to our principle that there is always more than one means to an end, we should ask what the alternatives may be. We would then need a definition of "a better life." This definition will be very different, however, in different cultures. Some will focus on material goods, others on maintaining traditions and an environment they care for, others again on the liberty to speak freely. Obviously, all cultures must make their own definition. For the first world to speak for all others, deciding that a good life is identical with economic, materialistic growth and modern technology, is to show disrespect for these cultural differences.

Second, "a better life" is different for a lion and an arctic fox. They fit into different niches, they feel happy under different conditions. Under what conditions does man feel happy? Generally, research on quality of life indicates that as long as basic needs are met, factors other than material ones seem to be the more important. These are factors such as belonging, security, meaningful work, being able to influence one's own situation, and self-realization. From an ecological point of view, this should not be surprising. As we saw in Chapter 14, where we discussed ecologically sound working environments, man also is adapted to a niche, or a way of life. Although man is ever so flexible, it is still rather far-fetched to think that there should be no limits to the environments he can create for himself and still feel happy.[1] Man is naturally, genetically adapted to smaller units, a life in less complicated societies, with less alienating technology, with more nature around him, with more time to enjoy it, and with fewer material possessions than the mean in industrial societies. This is his natural niche, which industrial man should begin to rebuild, instead of tearing it apart even more. According to this line of thought, material, economic growth is definitely not the only and the best means of obtaining "a better life."

This being the case, possible negative growth and a lowering of the level of material consumption in the rich, industrialized countries should not be seen as an environmentally motivated sacrifice. It would, of course, contribute to the circumvention of an ecological disaster. But instead of defining it as a necessary evil, we should see it as an opportunity for rediscovering our lost values. In fact, we can define the lowering of material consumption in the first world as something we do to increase our own quality of life!

Industrial man needs ecological change, whatever the findings of the imagined worldwide expert group. He has a need to rebuild an environment more like his natural niche. We could in fact speak of a psychological and sociological eco-crisis, besides the physiochemical one.

To prevent any misunderstandings: There is every reason to believe that a worldwide material (physiochemical) eco-crisis is a reality. The most important components are global warming, damage of the ozone layer, deforestation, desertification and soil erosion, pollution and extensive over-use of water, polluted air and water, acid rain, loss of species, population growth, and overtaxing of a diversity of resources.[2] *A special class of problems is the amount of risk factors man now handles. Every day new chemicals are developed and put to use. New developments in the area of biotechnology exacerbate the problem. The interactions between all these factors raise the amount to an unknown Xth power. Even with very low risks for each risk factor, the sum of all risks and their possible interactions is disturbing.*

For the majority of the world's population, other reflections and conclusions must be stated than those stated for the people in the first world. Not having the essential minimums for life implies a need for development and a striving for higher living standards. The need for ecological change then takes on different forms and should receive different local solutions in the respective countries spread over the four worlds.

The driving forces behind the eco-crises are partly activities linked to economic, materialistic growth in the industrial countries, partly similar activities driven by the same forces in the developing countries. Other driving forces are poverty and population growth in developing countries leading to short-sighted action for survival.

To conclude: *There is an accelerating, worldwide, psychological, sociological, and material eco-crisis which constitutes an emergency situation. It calls for immediate ecological change, with different local contents.*

CONSIDERATIONS AND VALUES

To think ecologically is to think holistically. Chapter 3 armed us with knowledge of the fundamental regularities of natural ecosystems. But a holistic view also should address the whole paradigm of ecology. The implicit *values* of an ecological worldview are presented below.

By the end of our century, industrial man will be in a historically new position. He will have more information than ever before in history, on nature, man and his history, technology, and culture. He will know more about the universe and about the anthropological diversity humans have built, mainly through the last 10,000 years. He has seen, and can imagine, the whole globe seen from the outside, from space. He can adopt a mental third position to mankind. (Whether he is more intelligent in his fourth position than man of ten thousand years ago, I don't know. Let us hope so.)

Ornstein and Ehrlich give a telling picture of man in earth's history. In their book *New World New Mind,* they ask us to imagine Earth's history as a year's calendar. It starts at midnight on January 1, New Year's eve one year later is today. On this time line bacteria appear in February. Fishes appear about November 20, dinosaurs about December 10. Our first ancestors appear on the scene in the afternoon of December 31. Homo Sapiens would be there at about 11:45 P.M., one-quarter of an hour before New Year's eve—today![3] The age of technology and industry, we might add, would last less than a second in this year-long earth's history. I see this perspective as a cornerstone in the ecological paradigm. This perspective calls for humility. Most of us expect a newcomer in the class, in the neighborhood, or at work to show some humble interest for the traditions and institutions. A new boss who tells everyone what they should do in the first minutes on the job shows ignorance and incompetence. But industrial man can be seen as such a person, who thinks he knows best after one second's experience.

The duty to consider future generations now is a matter of constant discussion among environmentally aware people. But what do we mean by future generations? How far should our calendar for "next year" go? If future generations means the next hundred years, the situation is not too dramatic. If it means another 300,000 years, that we are now halfway to the end of man's history, that is, that 10,000 generations are to follow us, then it is time to reconsider!

It also is a fact that scientific truths do not last forever. A hundred years ago science prescribed a stay in the centrifuge to cure psychosis, and lobotomy was practiced until recently as a good cure. Antibiotics were regarded as the final victory over bacteria, the invisible arms race between bacteria and antibiotic came as a frightening surprise to the optimistic researchers. Chemicals that were said to be "totally harmless" have turned out not to be so. One hundred fifty years ago, leading scientists rejected Semmelweiss's findings about the prophylactic use of antiseptics. Now his findings represent mainstream science. DDT was praised as the pesticide that would solve the health problems of huge populations. Today we know that it should never have been produced at all. Order in chaos is becoming a scientific truth. "Nature . . . is neither transparent, previsible, manipulable, nor stable, and humans (scientists) must cease to consider themselves as 'objective' observers out of time and space. . . . Rationality has lost its privilege of having direct access to the truth, i.e., of objectivity and neutrality," says Marc Luyckx.[4]

The world is a complicated place, the effects of our activities often cross professional borders. For example, traditional communities based on mixed agriculture, and mostly self-sufficient, may profit economically from a change to specialized operation. But the impact of the changes easily crosses over to the domains of sociology, health, and psychology. These are rarely considered by the planning economists and engineers: Yearly celebrations and rituals connected with the traditional way of operation may be lost. Social institutions break down and social and health-related misery results. In fact, this is more of a rule than an exception in projects for development in the third and fourth worlds. These considerations, together with what we learned from the ecosystem, are the background for the following discussion of the ecological path.

At one level, sole reasoning ends and aesthetics and ethics begin. Norms and values are implicit in any argument or opinion. I find it appropriate to state them explicitly for the sake of clarification. Three values are proposed here as significant and right in themselves. I believe that most people share them. At the same time, different implications or norms can be drawn from them. The values are:

1. Nature has intrinsic value.

2. Mankind has intrinsic value.

3. Individual and social happiness have intrinsic value.

NATURE HAS INTRINSIC VALUE

Everything in nature has the same point of origin, everything is interconnected, everything is kindred: All nature's organisms are our relatives and Mother Earth is our common home. This is one way of understanding this value. Another is that we share destiny: Without nature there would be no humans. Whatever the reasoning, we have to conclude that nature has intrinsic value. In all known cultures, through all times, man has experienced a meaningful existence, aesthetics, or general happiness with nature: The smell of the pines, the sound of heavy swell, the sight of a wild cat, the silence of deep woods, the drama of arctic winters! Most religious breakthroughs happen in man's encounter with Mother Nature.

Nature, then, is our home that we should take care of, our source of experience of beauty which we should take care of, our basis for life as we know human forms of life up to now, which we should also take care of, as well as our bank account given to us by our parents, for us to hand on to our children and their successors to the end of time.

In his proposal for a platform for Deep Ecology, Arne Naess, one of our leading "ecosophers" argues that:

1. The flourishing of human and non-human life on Earth has inherent value. The value of non-human life-forms is independent of the usefulness of the non-human world for human purposes.

2. The richness and diversity of life-forms are also values in themselves and contribute to the flourishing of human and non-human life on earth.

3. Humans have no right to reduce this richness and diversity except to satisfy vital needs.[5]

As I have shown, an essential feature of stable ecosystems is biodiversity. This carries a beauty of its own, and is a precondition for securing nature. Nature's battlefield for survival is the ecosystems. From this value, and the elaborations we have made, we can then draw these norms:

1a. Large tracts of virgin land should be preserved!

1b. Biodiversity should be preserved!

1c. All parts of the environment should be exploited, preserved, or rebuilt with reverence!

MANKIND HAS INTRINSIC VALUE

The statement that nature and mankind share destiny is a semi-truth. Nature in fact can do well without us, we cannot do without nature. A Norwegian eco-philosopher, Peter Wessel Zappfe, was of the opinion that a global human suicide is needed to save the planet from our destruction. (But in this way, leaving our first position completely seems to be an unrealistic demand.)

As I see it, "mankind" should not mean *as many* people as possible. Nor should it mean a certain number. Neither in the context of ecosystems nor in the context of mankind should industrial man play God. We have no right to decide that mankind should mean seven billion or three billion, or even today's about five billion. What it should mean is that we take responsibility for caring for ourselves and others, and for the environment that all societies depend on.

The diversity of cultures is a fundamental characteristic of mankind as we know it. No person belonging to one culture has the right or the competence to compare cultures and rank one as better than another. "Mankind" here should signify diversity, without bias by industrial man toward modern "democracies," "dynamic economies," or other features of his particular society. Over thousands of years, cultural evolution has brought forth cultures more diverse than any other species could ever dream of. The adaptation of life's different cultural forms to their local environment bears the same beauty as nature itself. Arne Naess, again: "It would, in my view, be a cultural disaster for mankind if one philosophy or one religion were to become established on earth. It would be a disaster if future Green Societies were so similar that they blocked the development of deep cultural differences."[6] Let us further add a few words from the eco-philosopher Henryk Skolimowski: "Thus if we want to preserve and maintain a thriving life, whether of an ecological habitat, of a culture, or of an individual, diversity is a *sine qua non*. As such, it is our *moral responsibility* to maintain and increase diversity.[7] As a matter of fact, one could say that culture is an aspect of nature, that we should think man-in-nature and not man-above-nature. To preserve the diversity of cultures is a noble task. Let us then derive two norms from this value:

2a. Mankind's eternal existence should be sustained!

2b. Anthropological diversity should be maintained!

INDIVIDUAL AND SOCIAL HAPPINESS HAVE INTRINSIC VALUE

To industrial man, the question of happiness has become complicated. His bewilderment is spread worldwide through modern media. At the core of his bewilderment lies his confusion of *living standard* with *quality of life*. With living standard I here refer to how many material goods he can afford, whereas quality of life signifies his degree of subjective happiness. It seems to be clear now that, in general, there is a low correlation between the two. It also seems as if all individuals, and all communities, have to find their own way and create their own standards.

Let us elaborate on this: From 1946 to 1978 living standards in the United States rose rapidly. However, indicators of SWB (subjective well-being) showed no increase whatsoever! The indicators that do covary with SWB are inconsistent and disputable. The conclusion to be drawn is: As long as the basic human needs are minimally met, do not increases in the living standard lead to increase in quality of life.[8]

However, we can make some generalizations. There is less mental poverty, delinquency, and destructive conflict in cultures that are left undisturbed. Happiness or cultural identity cannot be imported. Development assistance to so-called underdeveloped countries runs an overwhelming risk of troublemaking contrary to its good intentions. Human communities share some characteristics with ecosystems: They are complex and self-organizing systems. The idea of "developing" a culture from the top or the outside carries as little aesthetics as the idea of "developing" an ecosystem.

The characteristic of self-sufficiency is another fundamental topic. Most ecosystems are to a high degree self-sufficient. This could serve as an ideal also for cultural stability and identity. Only through independence from the international unstable markets can local cultures become stabilized. John Maynard Keynes said: "Ideas, knowledge, art, hospitality, travel—these are the things which should of their nature be international. But let goods be homespun whenever it is reasonably and conveniently possible; and above all, let finance be primarily national.[9] In our ecological perspective, finance is not the most important factor to keep national or local. But the production of goods in general should be as local as possible.

In the light of environmental threats, this also has another relevance. Let us make an experiment of thought: A community is to decide how much and what kind of energy it will spend. It has to place the source of energy in the middle of its own community, and accept the environmental costs also of producing the source. Would it choose nuclear power? Coal-fired power plants? First and foremost, it would choose to spend as little energy as possible. Second, it would choose the cleanest possible source with lowest level of risk. The reason for these choices is that the consequences would be visible or directly experienced. Feedback loops of positive and negative feedback would be established. The community would thereby have a chance to take sustainable decisions.

For man to experience happiness, he should experience meaning, security, and belonging. Again, these are not "things" that can be supplied to the individual. They are values that the individual should be given the chance to create for himself. What we can do is avoid placing obstacles in the way of this happening. I propose these norms based on the values discussed:

3a. Communities should not be hindered in finding their own way!

3b. Communities should be based mainly on self-sufficiency!

3c. Individuals should not be hindered in finding their own way!

3d. Meaning, security, and belonging should not be taken away from the individual!

How controversial should we suppose these values and norms to be? Not very, I assume. (Norm 3b *is* controversial. See Appendix 4 for a broad discussion.) So, why all this fuss about it? It is because the international development can take different paths, with dramatically different results for us and the coming generations. It will take conscious and strong decisions to bring about the desired course. Not least, it will take a considerable degree of insight and consciousness from business and industry's decision makers. That is why we have to state the obvious, or bring it out into the open. "How would mankind's present role on this planet be evaluated in the light of philosophical worldviews of the past?" asks Arne Naess, and continues:

No matter which one of the great philosophies one considers to be valid, our current role would be evaluated negatively. It is in opposition to value priority as announced by these philosophies. This applies to Aristotelianism, Buddhism, Confucianism, and other great philosophies of the last two millennia. In the great philosophies, greatness and bigness are differentiated. Greatness is sought, but it is not magnitude. The importance of technology is recognized, but cultural values get priority of consideration. The good life is not made dependent upon thought-less consumption. . . . My conclusion is that there is no articulate world-view which endorses mankind's current role in the ecosphere. Environmentalism has no artic-ulated philosophical system to fear.[10]

LOCAL PRODUCTION FOR LOCAL CONSUMPTION FOR LOCAL RECIRCULATION

I have formulated a universal line to be drawn on the basis of these values and ethical norms, ecosystems theory, and experiences from inter-national aid programs and business: *Local production for local consump-tion for local recirculation.* Let us now elaborate on this slogan.

Environmentalists often claim that "eco-problems cannot be solved lo-cally, since they are global by nature." This parole should be analyzed carefully, since it is the root of much confusion. Very few eco-problems are truly global in the sense that the consequences of local actions are global, that is, affect the whole globe. This only goes for depletion of the ozone layer and for global warming. A whole lot of eco-problems are transnational in the sense that other countries than the one causing the eco-problems are affected. Problems like some cases of pollution of air and water, nuclear radiation, acid rain, and overtaxing of certain migrating species belong to this category. Population growth, desertification, soil ero-sion, and poverty are also eco-problems of transnational character when they cause migration. However, most eco-problems, in the broad sense of the word applied here, are of a local kind.

Truly global problems take global solutions. It is a noble task for the UN and all nations of the world individually to work for and to secure the success of such solutions. But global solutions are unlikely to succeed. This is illustrated by the helplessness of the UN to solve international conflicts. Surveys of the effect of international, environmental agreements are not promising. The Montreal protocol, signed in 1987 and followed up by specified directives, shows this for one. Only 23% of the 131 countries that signed it have followed it up in practice. When it comes to costs, most countries seem to put balancing their national budgets before international obligations. It is important that only the truly global eco-problems are tagged "global." If an all-inclusive eco-problem is to be solved by the UN, our chances to succeed are close to zero.

Transnational eco-problems must be solved through negotiations be-tween the countries involved. Other nations, international courts of justice, and international conventions should be drawn on as resources for conflict solving. Local eco-problems should be solved by the people experiencing them, who have local cultural belonging and insight.

Ecosystems and local cultures cannot and should not be "managed" as a "global" unit. They are too complex, and too many interest groups always will press for bad compromises. Nobody can represent a fair third position and thereby exhibit adequate leadership. Feedback becomes too complex, the consequences do not reach the right recipient.

Global management of a global ecosystem and the possible gradual development of a global monoculture are especially frightening in the age of advanced technology, not least biotechnology. Industrial man has proven beyond doubt that he is unable to handle his scientific toys with the necessary caution. Man's political and social systems are unstable and shifting. For instance, we have not succeeded in our attempts to eliminate war. The global ecosystem may exist for millions of years still, if given the chance to self-organize. Shifting political regimes and scientific "truths" simply cannot be trusted with the task of managing "the global ecosystems."

Another danger is that a "globalizing" of eco-problems leads to solutions that are satisfactory for the industrial world at the cost of others. The influence on decisions is unevenly distributed. The idea of global commons, where the resources in the near future may be seen as the property of all mankind is frightening, seen from the perspective of small nations, from developing countries, and especially from the fourth world's point of view. The smallest or least-developed countries, which are made dependent on goodwill from the rich world, will lose out in all negotiations on the "global commons."

A global strategy to solve the eco-problems, then, is a set-up for failure. We need international conventions which place limitations on the nations' right to pollute and tax resources that are international. We need a world police force, or other means to enforce these agreements. But further expansions from this minimum are doomed to fail.

The rich world has a double moral duty to help the developing countries solve their eco-problems. First it is the duty to help one's neighbors in distress. Second, the first world bears the obligation of the one who, historically speaking, has caused many of the problems. The cultural imbalance, overpopulation, and health problems of the developing countries have been caused mainly by European and North American colonialism, imperialism, and industrialization over the last hundred years. But the duty to help is not the duty to give wrong medicine or medicine which has unpredictable consequences. For help to really be help, it has to be adapted to the local culture with absolute respect and with an altruistic motivation. Instead, industrial countries again and again prescribe for these problems the medicine of technical and medical megaprojects based on the cultural premises of the first world, and based on the motive of profit.

In his classic from 1973, E. F. Schumacher argues for a parallel conclusion, which is still relevant. In developing countries, he argues, four propositions for sound development should be met:

—Work places should be created where people are actually living
—Work places should be cheap enough to be independent of large-scale financial investments
—Simple production methods should be applied, which do not demand high skills, complex organization, a large amount of raw materials, marketing efforts, and capital
—Production should be based on local materials and delivery to local customers.[11]

Local solving of local eco-problems is the most realistic way. Transnational eco-problems should be punctuated as locally as possible and solved as locally as possible. Transnational aid on local cultural premises is to be desired. Local production for local consumption for local recirculation is the desired direction. It cannot suddenly become a reality. It cannot be decided by a government or a group of investors. It should be the consequence of a new ecological consciousness among consumers, interest groups, investors, and politicians over a long period of time. It cannot be a definite state of affairs, it should be read as "as local as realistically possible and desirable." Local production for local consumption for local recirculation is an overriding, long-term ecological ideal.

Chapter 20

Business Ethics in the Age of Ecology

> Good ethics is profitable because it creates confidence amongst owners, personnel, customers, authorities, politicians, journalists and the general public. Like artists, business leaders should attach as much importance to the ethical dimension of their actions (content) as the aesthetical (form), and try to obtain a comfortable balance between the two.
> Bengt Rydén, Foreword to Tad Tuleja, *Beyond the Bottom Line*

THE INTEREST GROUPS

No large business can expect to win credibility these days if pure profit is the only aim. Credence demands more highly developed ethics—in writing, in speech, and in practice. In our contemporary information society, we get to know about the businesses' ethical standards and their practice much more quickly than before. We can indicate six relevant, interrelated interest groups, all of which stand to gain from common ethical rules:

The local community will cooperate with the company if it is revealed as being an ethically reliable partner. For example, companies with a respectable practice on taxpaying, work places, and environment will gain support.

The company owners will show an interest in the running of the company as well as an interest in its development, if they perceive it as both financially sound and ethically worthy. It is estimated that about 10% of all investments made in the United States today are ethically motivated.[1] Ethical investment has increased throughout the last twenty years, and environmental concerns weigh in heavily.

The company employees will commit themselves to the company even more if its ethical reputation is high. They will identify with the company, defend it in the market, and in this way be the company's strongest advocates.

The company's suppliers will fulfill their obligations and support the company as its ethical standard rises.

The company's customers will show a growing solidarity with the ethically sound company. They will have confidence that they receive the deserved service, and they will advocate the company's products and be strong spokesmen for the company.

The company's competitors will perceive the company as trustworthy when it shows a strong ethical profile, and they will go for win-win solutions in situations of "opposing interests."

The company that wins the confidence of the six interest groups gains several long-term, competitive advantages. Even in periods where it is inferior with regard to product, service, or price, the support gained from the six groups may enable it to survive.

From an ecological point of view, we can add some interest groups that can hardly speak for themselves, but will have spokesmen among the public:

Coming generations will be represented by socially aware people from all the mentioned interest groups.

The local/regional physiochemical environment will be represented by authorities, public opinion, environmentalists, and, of course, the stated interest groups.

The global ecosystems, including man, other species, and the physiochemical environment, will also be represented in these groups.

The potential gain for the company by obtaining the support of all these groups is tremendous. But high ethics in proclamation and action, based primarily on egoistic motives, is too weak a foundation for business and industry to build on. We can in fact claim that this represents a primitive first stage along an imagined ethical development path, which we now will explore further.

ETHICS AND DEVELOPMENT THEORY

The same actions can have different reasons and, based on these reasons, we can appoint differing ethical standards to the operators. Take, for example, a company that decides to launch its products in cartons made from recycled materials. The decision can be made on the grounds that the market has become environmentally aware, and that it would be profitable for the company to acquire a green profile, or the decision can be based on a genuine concern for environmental issues, and the company may even be prepared to accept a loss for contributing to a cleaner environment.

New economist Paul Ekins says: "Companies can decide to reduce their environmental impact for many reasons: a commitment at top management level to a clean, sustainable future; the avoidance of financial penalties and bad publicity; a perceived competitive advantage; to save money by using resources more efficiently and reducing wastes; to respond to pressure-group and public opinion; to keep ahead of legislation; to be good corporate citizens; or the belief that good management includes good environmental management."[2]

The respective grounds can be said to be expressions of differing degrees of ethical maturity. When we move from judgement of actions to judgement of grounds for action, we enter the area of moral reasoning. It is not enough to simply have ethical standards; all rules have their exceptions. Even the standard "you shall not tell lies" can be annulled during wartime interrogation. Justifiable reclaim of stolen goods can annul the standard "you shall not steal." Justifiable warfare can annul the standard "you shall not kill." In many cases, the moral reasoning will be decisive in judging an operator's ethical standard.

Moral actions that are motivated solely to satisfy one's own needs, or to avoid punishment, represent the least-developed stage, viewed in light of a developmental perspective on moral reasoning. Willingness to adapt to common social standards, and the will to contribute to socially constructive actions can be said to represent the next stage. Willingness to act with reciprocity and altruism, and loyalty to one's own ethical standards and values, even at the expense of negative consequences for oneself, can be said to be the most advanced stage.[3]

Model for three levels of moral reasoning:

Level 1: The operator holds profit for himself (possibly also for close relatives) as the grounds for his actions. Material gain and avoidance of punishment are crucial.

Level 2: The operator holds that which is socially and legally right or wrong as the grounds for his actions. The gaining of social acceptance combined with loyal conformity is crucial.

Level 3: The operator holds his own standard of right and wrong as grounds for his actions. Self-respect with regard to his own ethical standards is crucial.

Let us consider an example of a situation that is ethically challenging, and see how this is expressed. A company has been storing special, environmentally dangerous waste in drums at a remote site for many years. The storage is irresponsible but cheap. The dump is discovered by environmental activists who contact the management. The management works out plans for responsible storage in record time, and implements them in cooperation with an environmental organization. At the same time, they start a comprehensive revision of their production methods with the focus on environment friendliness. The management is active in getting press coverage and general media attention and acquires a pronounced green profile.

These actions could have all the above levels of moral reasoning as grounds. If the action is motivated solely by the wish to profit the company, with the green profile as aid, it belongs to level 1. The grounds could also be that society expects green behavior, and has instituted laws to ensure this. Compliance and adherence to these codes as grounds put it at level 2. If the grounds for the actions are an independent attitude toward ecological problems and a genuine desire to contribute in a positive manner, based on an assessment of the impending environmental threat, then the grounds belong to level 3.

Is the level 3 of moral reasoning at all relevant to business? One author answers the question this way: "Business does not have an obligation to protect the environment over and above what is required by the law; however, it does have a moral obligation to avoid intervening in the political arena in order to defeat or weaken environmental legislation."[4] Others have argued that it is essential, for the capitalist system to function, that business retreat from any deeper ethical and social engagement. The conclusion then again is: Stick to business profitability and leave the responsibility for social and environmental conditions to the legal authorities and the politicians.

I have two major objections to this point of view. First, I see free capitalism as an ideal system perhaps to be reached in the far future. No society fully lets loose all capitalist forces; some degree of governmental steering is always involved. The main reason is that industry and business are not sufficiently ethically developed to be able to handle the ideal unlimited freedom. Hence, for free capitalism to work, *more* ethics and *more* encompassing ethics are needed! Second, when it comes to ecological problems, we have an emergency situation. In this situation all bodies must take broad ethical responsibility and join forces. Business and industry are too important to be excepted from this general state of affairs.

In the internationalized and sharpened competitive situation currently experienced by the business community, the ethical dilemmas become even more problematic. We must remember that every private business's existence depends on its return on invested capital, and by virtue of its profitability. This exerts a pressure on any business exclusively in the direction of level 1. But business and industry must not limit their contributions solely to profitable actions, based on level 1 moral reasoning. New opportunities for profit with environmentally unwanted impact will emerge. The exploitation of these opportunities will replace the greening of business very soon, if the moral reasoning is entrenched only at level 1. Environmentalism then may "go out of fashion!"

ETHICS AND PUNCTUATION

Business and the interest groups need firm ethical standards from which they do not depart. We need a set of general ethical minimum standards that serious business people in any normal situation can be expected to follow—irrespective of the underlying reasoning. This is the same as a society needing common law and order. Examples of such standards are:

Abiding with the law. Any company should follow the laws and regulations imposed on it by legal bodies.

Correct information. All interest groups are entitled to truthful information; while essential information is neither omitted nor concealed.

Keeping of agreements. All interest groups are entitled to binding verbal and written agreements, legal or otherwise.

Reciprocity. All interest groups are entitled to a reasonable degree of reciprocity in that neither information, the situation, nor position is abused in order to gain an unfair advantage or create undue obstacles for others.

Incorruptibility. All interest groups are entitled to unambiguous roles, and that no one be subjected to a conflict of loyalties by means of direct or indirect bribery.

Confidentiality. All interest groups are entitled to confidentiality with regard to information given in confidence.

Such standards normally cannot be "bent." If emergency situations give rise to reconsideration, any deviance should be based on moral reasoning totally free from any personal gain, that is, based on level 2 or 3 of moral reasoning.

But let us then introduce a little relativity into the arena. A boy steals money from a shop. The action is unethical according to the commandment "thou shalt not steal." But let us broaden our punctuation: The boy has a sister who is ill and needs an expensive operation if she is to avoid lifelong suffering. He steals to finance the operation. The theft is then an *altruistic* theft. The action suddenly becomes ethical according to the commandment "help thy neighbor." But then we broaden the punctuation even further: Others get to hear about the action. The commandment "thou shalt not steal" is undermined. The action helps to break down ethical standards at community level. The action becomes once more unethical according to a standard that might read "you shall fully support community ethics in all that you do." And so on (Figure 20.1). Ethics at the higher levels of a hierarchy of system levels (the more comprehensive delimitations) must come first—but cannot totally omit the subordinate levels! And no deviation should be made from the enduring ethical standards. A noble end does not excuse unethical means.

The example illustrates how the sum of good actions (help thy neighbor)

Figure 20.1
**Example of an Ethical Dilemma as It Emerges When Different Punctuations
Are Applied**

Society over a long time: "Support community ethics" => Don't steal!
Boy + familiy over time: "Help thy neighbor" => Steal!
Boy in shop here and now: "Thou shall not steal" => Don't steal!

at one level can give destructive results (breakdown of standards in society) at a higher level in the hierarchy of system levels. This represents a striking parallel to the tragedy of the commons mentioned earlier. A nation may punctuate its own needs for industrial growth as priority number one, gaining its wanted rise in living standards, but costing the commons, for instance, a rise in carbon dioxide emissions. At the hierarchical level it decides on, the decision is a sound one. At a higher level, the sum of all countries doing this may be disastrous. In that case, the activity is unethical. Consideration of the whole must override consideration of the part. Consideration of a long-term, ecologically sound development must override consideration of any short-term profit for individuals or companies. When international environmental protection clashes with short-term and local business interests, the environmental considerations must be given first priority. These considerations are governing and overriding even when the business opportunities could have given badly needed jobs or other benefits.

ETHICAL ECOLOGICAL STANDARDS IN BUSINESS

Every age has its age-typical problems which will have hierarchical precedence above all others. If we look at Western Europe and North America, unemployment and depression were perhaps the dominant problems between the two world wars. During World War II, the problem was the fight (seen from the allies' position) against Nazi fascism. After the war the dominant picture was peacekeeping, with special emphasis on avoiding nuclear conflict. Standards for international human aid became increasingly ethically more fundamental during the 1970s. What now?

The serious position in which the world finds itself with regard to the ecological crisis has necessitated the designation of ecological ethics as being the highest priority in the field of ethical problems. It has been established beyond doubt that business and industry play a decisive part in the set of environmental problems we face today. Ecological considerations should have an ethical precedence for at least one further generation in most places in the world. This should serve as a general guideline when ethical dilemmas emerge. James Otter, by the Nordic division of ICI, describes one such dilemma: "After lengthy debate in parliament the Indian government decided to approve the sale and use of DDT in India for use in malaria control programs. However, DDT is banned in developed countries. Trade in DDT to India by a corporation could therefore be categorized as a form of double standard, and therefore against many corporate philosophies. Alternatively, the decision not to supply could be classed as a racist decision and contrary to the profit objectives of the company, by imposing standards contrary to local law."[5]

According to the argument presented here, the ecological considerations should be overriding and weigh heavier than all other considerations. This goes in favor of not selling DDT to any customer. Sticking to its principle, "never sell DDT," and our ideal of local self-organizing and self-sufficiency, the company in question could sell its know-how to the Indian government to solve the problem in the most ecologically sound manner.

In our discussion on the ecological path, some values were declared and nine norms were formulated. They were:

1. Nature has intrinsic value.

1a. Large tracts of virgin land should be preserved!

1b. Biodiversity should be preserved!

1c. All parts of the environment should be exploited, preserved, or rebuilt with reverence!

2. Mankind has intrinsic value.

2a. Mankind's eternal existence should be sustained!

2b. Anthropological diversity should be maintained!

3. Individual and social happiness have intrinsic value.

3a. Communities should not be hindered in finding their own way!

3b. Communities should be based mainly on self-sufficiency!

3c. Individuals should not be hindered in finding their own way!

3d. Meaning, security, and belonging should not be taken away from the individual!

For business the relevance of these norms varies somewhat. Points 1a. to 1c. place direct bonds on the business actors. Activity threatening biodiversity is unethical. The status of nature as virgin land, and local or national plans for such tracts, should be respected. Lobbying, or other methods to bypass this are unethical. In general, all production should show respect for the environment in its broadest sense. This is also in accordance with Principle 6 of the Business Charter for Sustainable Development (BCSD) from ICC (International Chamber of Commerce).

This states that products and services should be offered which "have no undue environmental impact and are safe in their intended use, that are efficient in their consumption of energy and natural resources, and that can be recycled, reused, or disposed of safely." It also is in accordance with their Principle 10, which instructs business to apply a precautionary approach "to prevent serious or irreversible environmental degradation."[6]

Norm 2a. implies that all scientific research that threatens mankind in any way is unethical. This represents a complicated discussion which will not be included here. Let me only emphasize that the globe is our heirloom, which we should safeguard and respect forever.

The norm of anthropological diversity represents a challenge to all international business and industry, as do the four last norms, derived from the value of individual and social happiness. (For a general discussion, see Appendix 4.)

Proponents for deep ecology have advocated that the seriousness of the ecological situation calls for exceptional actions. Business should join forces with the environmentalists and others, and not see itself as a passive follower of governmental action and lawmaking. It should see itself as a key contributor to an ecologically sound future for generations to come. Business should join forces with all interest groups in this matter. It should follow and advocate enduring ethical standards and ecological ethical norms. Individual businesses should strive to raise their level of moral reasoning, both internally and among the external interest groups. When ethical paradoxes emerge, they should give priority to the larger punctuation and to the ecological aspects.

ECOLOGICALLY SOUND PROFIT IN FOUR WORLDS

So far our reflections have been of a general nature. But the different worlds have different needs, provide different opportunities, and raise different ethical demands.

The first world: The environmentally aware business and industry of the first world should here contribute to the development and implementation of:

—local production for local consumption for local recirculation

—greening of "business as usual"

—green technology

—green energy

—waste management

—environmental restoration programs

—a general shift away from material consumption toward environmentally friendly servies, services enhancing quality of life, art and culture, and generally avoid contributing to an unreasonable growth in material consumption

The second world: The environmentally aware business and industry of the first world should here contribute to the development and implementation of:

—local production for local consumption for local recirculation

—greening of "business as usual"

—green technology

—green energy

—waste management

—environmental restoration programs

Financial investments should be based on principles of cultural respect.

The third world: The environmentally aware business and industry of the first world should here contribute to the development and implementation of:

—local production for local consumption for local recirculation

—greening of "business as usual" when business already exists

—green technology when technology already exists

—green energy to the degree that energy already is exploited

—waste management when waste problems exist

—environmental restoration programs

Financial investments should be based on principles of cultural respect. For all categories "development" should be limited and not be forced on the society. Traditional methods of production should be supported, not eliminated.

The fourth world: The environmentally aware business and industry of the first world should here contribute to the development and implementation of:

—environmental restoration programs

Apart from this, business could best contribute by staying away.

CHECK YOUR COMPANY: ETHICS

• Does your company deserve and receive support from all the interest groups?

• To which degree are the employees' actions motivated by

    1. A wish to profit personally, and to avoid punishment

    2. A wish to comply with company rules

    3. A wish to follow own standards for right and wrong

• To which degree is your company greening to

    1. Gain a direct profit and avoid legal prosecution

    2. Comply with social standards and the legislation

    3. Contribute altruistically to an ecologically sound future

• Does your company uphold the enduring ethical standards in all relations internally and externally?

• When ecological considerations conflict with other temporal considerations, do you give the ecological considerations priority?

• Are local conditions regarded and respected when your company operates in different districts, countries, or parts of the world?

CHECK YOURSELF: ETHICS

• Apply the questions above to yourself.

Part VI

Profit, Ethics, and Eco-Problems

Growth for the sake of growth itself is the ideology of cancer cells.

Anonymous

Chapter 21

Green, Ethical, and Profitable

The greening of Europe (North America, Asia) is, have no doubt, a matchless opportunity for the wise corporation. It is not a threat!
Tom Peters, in M.S. Haskins, *The Greening of European Business*

SCALING ECOLOGICAL PERFORMANCE

A business's existence depends on its ability to give a return on invested capital. The business ethics set the rules of the game. The ecological challenge indicates a desired direction for business involvement. This might be seen merely as consisting of barriers and obstacles, which I regret is the case for all too many businesses. But all medals have two sides. Through the filter of "business as usual," the age of ecology, with all its formal regulations and informal new rules, is perceived as a yoke. Through the filter of the futuristic investor and manager, an array of new opportunities emerges for every environmental change, even with every new regulation.

What are the relevant parameters for scaling of ecological performance? For one thing, when *Fortune* scores the environmental top ten, its number one, AT&T, gets its score because, since 1990, it has lowered emissions to air by 81%, cut disposal of waste in half, reduced CFCs by 86% (since 1986), recycled 60% of office paper, and used 10% less paper. It offers incentives to employees who propose actions for enhancing environmental performance, and produces a good annual environmental report.[1] As we see, this is a physiochemical evaluation, plus an appreciation of factors that can be placed into the categories of educating employees, customers, and suppliers. The scoring also took into consideration the degree to which the environment is regarded as a strategic focus area, as it is reflected in the production of an annual report.

The BCSD, in Principle 1, instructs business that "environmental management should be among the highest corporate priorities." Further, it expects business to educate employees, customers, contractors, and suppliers in environmental matters. Also, business's role as contributor to the general effort to "enhance environmental awareness and protection" is formulated. This truly is a praiseworthy project of considerable value.

To further broaden the perspective on an ecological scaling, let us summarize our ecological demands on the business community in an *ecological factor*. The higher the score for factors in the nominator (above the line), and the lower the score for factors in the denominator (below the line), the more ecologically sound the company.

Emergency preparedness
+ Safe disposal of residual waste
+ Ecology as strategic focus area
+ Waste sorting
+ Product and material recycling
+ Ecological education of customers and suppliers
+ Ecological education of employees
+ Ecologically sound products and services only
+ Green R&D
+ Ecologically sound working environments
+ Buying used and recycled equipment
+ Repairing and reusing usable equipment
+ Green business partners only
+ Local production & consumption & recycling
+ Altruistic contribution to general ecological efforts

Ecological factor = _____

Pollution
+ Amount of energy expended
+ Amount of materials expended
+ Taxation of irreplaceable raw materials
+ Taxation of virgin land
+ Taxation of biodiversity

To make agreeable parameters for all the elements in this factor is a difficult task. But the fact that it is difficult is no excuse. We should seek where the keys were lost, not where the light is strongest. The factor represents an ideal, and any improvement of your business's score should be welcomed. We are facing an international ecological turnaround in which business and industry play a decisive role. Any business in the world has the potential to develop in an ecological direction. All contributions should be welcomed, be they ever so small or ever so egoistically motivated.

ABIDING BY THE LAW AND CUTTING COSTS

Even decision makers who run their businesses by the idea of "business as usual" can contribute to the ecological turnaround that is needed. Any business should, at least for egoistical economic reasons, evaluate the amount of energy and materials it expends. Quantified goals should be set, such as British Gas does: "Our target is to achieve a 15 per cent saving in energy costs by the end of 1997, worth around £10 million per year."[2] Emergency preparedness and safe disposal of residual waste may be based solely on selfish economic reasoning, since they impliy prevention of possible costs connected with accidents.

The minimizing of all kinds of pollution is a matter of course, since it is becoming increasingly subject to legislation and restrictions. Monsanto Company was early out: "The Environmental Protection Agency recently announced final rules to reduce toxic air emissions of organic chemicals by almost 90 percent. Monsanto has had an aggressive, voluntary waste reduction program in place since 1988 when the company announced a goal to reduce toxic air emissions from its operations by 90 percent by the end of 1992. As of the end of 1992, the company had reduced its rate of emissions by 92 percent worldwide, and 85 percent in the United States from 1987 levels, five years earlier than the laws require."[3]

So, the gain from this kind of ecological change lies mainly in direct cost cutting and prevention of expenditures. At the same time, all these actions can be used to profile the company as green. As Canon Europe does: "We were one of the first companies to react to early scientific warnings about chlorolfluorocarbons (CFCs). As a result, we will eliminate CFSc in our manufacturing process by 1993, well ahead of schedule. Plus, we will phase out the use of methyl chloroform by the end of 1994, three years ahead of our original target. Our new products have environmental safety, well in excess of official standards, built-in from the beginning. We've virtually eliminated ozone emissions from our new copier range, while also making them considerably quieter and cutting down on energy consumption. Our recycling program has received worldwide acclaim."[4]

The gain then also lies in a potentially strengthened position in the market. The third gain lies in access to the emerging green networks. Companies, to an ever-stronger degree, put green demands on their collaborators. It is an advantage to be green enough for acceptance into all networks.

PLAIN GREENING OF BUSINESS

Ecology as strategic focus area represents a further and more advanced step. For those businesses who want to go further, yearly reports on environmental initiatives will separate them from those who lag behind. There is room for ecological considerations in all the elements of a business strategy (see Appendix 3).

Waste sorting will be practiced, even if it may not be directly profitable by itself. However, it will contribute to the green profile. These businesses also will demand something from others: They will apply the principle of ecological education of customers and suppliers. "In February 1991, Richard M. Carpenter, S.C. Johnson's president and chief executive officer, hosted an environmental symposium entitled 'Partners working for a better world,' which was attended by 57 of the company's top 70 supplier organizations supporting one or more of the company's business. The conference included presentations by well-known representatives of the global environmental, governmental and business communities." The discussions in the working groups focused on biodegradation, source reduction, recycling, and volatile organic compounds.[5] "AT&T has a policy of simply not accepting any packaging materials that are manufactured using CFCs. It is also requesting that its suppliers of components and equipment phase out their use of CFCs in materials sold to AT&T as soon as possible, but no later than 1994.[6]

Product and material recycling may not directly imply cost cutting, but will be practiced whether directly profitable or not. Here is an example: "We are reclaiming and remanufacturing about 1 million finished piece parts worldwide each year, representing a total value of approximately $200 million. Some 35% of the solid waste—approximately 6,500 tons— from our largest worldwide manufacturing site, in Webster, N.Y., is being either recycled or used as an alternative to fossil fuel. Significant quantities of solid waste are also being recycled at a growing number of other Xerox sites."[7]

Focus also needs to be held on the *internal* environment in business. An old proverb says: "Always sweep before your own door." Businesses that only contribute to the commons, and do not take their internal state of affairs into consideration, will hardly be taken seriously. The principle of education of employees represents one aspect of this. ICI, for instance, already spends large amounts of money on the environmental education of its co-workers at all levels. S.C. Johnson & Son established "Environmental Leadership Forums" in 1991, to educate mid to senior-level managers. DuPont has taken on strong initiatives; Dow Chemical, Waste

Management International, and many more do the same. Ecologically sound working environments will be an advantage that usually will pay directly. Businesses with such merit will attract the best employees, and the synergies of being of the best HR managers are many. The direct savings connected with good working environments also are considerable.

ECOLOGICAL PIONEERING

Limiting the taxation of irreplaceable raw materials can sometimes be a question of cutting costs. But the ecological pioneers also will prefer recycled material for ideal reasons. Such ecologically sound changes of business as these sometimes lead to net costs. And if the business takes even further steps along the ecological path, it may cost even more in a short-term punctuation: It may directly hinder potential business opportunities.

Taxation of biodiversity and taxation of virgin land are principles that may cause the environmentally aware decision maker to say no to profitable opportunities. The gains for businesses pioneering, with these advanced changes, will lie mainly in the realms of market profile. It will take bravery and a long-term perspective to dare to make these changes. At the same time, the potential cost savings in many of these areas are considerable, as a side effect.

The establishment of ecologically sound working environments should consider the physical, the psychological, and the social aspects, and green R&D should be directed at both the greening of existing products and the development of new and less environmentally costly products. The use of waste as raw material for new products is of great interest. Some years ago, the silicium producer Elkem in Norway was polluting the environment with about 150,000 tons of dust annually. New technology made it possible to separate 99% of the dust from the smoke before it spread into the environment. Today the dust, which is mixed into concrete to strengthen it, is exported to other countries in Europe and to the United States for a good profit. The use of waste and heat from production processes is taking on speed all over the world.

RADICAL ECOLOGICAL RETHINKING OF BUSINESS

If you consistently follow the principles of buying used and recycled equipment and of repairing and reusing usable equipment, then you break with one of our time's most unsound ideas: that new and expensive is better than cheap and used. You are giving priority to ecological values and it will be noticed in your environment. Your managers will drive used cars, you will have repairmen repairing equipment instead of throwing it away, your purchasing department will advertise for used office equipment, and you will be the last in the row to invest in new and fancy buildings.

The implementation of the principle of green business partners only (and/or educating them) will be practiced by business's radical rethinkers. Through such initiatives, those businesses will be the entrepreneurs of green networks. This may cost in the short run, but in the long run green networks will pay for the ones inside, while those outside will lose out.

As already mentioned, one fast-growing niche is the niche for products and services directed at greener production and transport, resulting in ecologically sound products and services. One objective for these products and services is less and cleaner energy-demanding processes. Another is less-polluting production processes. More economizing with irreplaceable raw materials is a third. The market for these products and services seems to be growing, even in times of general recession.

Waste recycling and waste management is another business niche of considerable dimensions. Asia is an example of a growing market. The World Bank has estimated that, for example, Thailand will spend $ 1.5 billion a year on environmental services by the year 2000. It is also estimated that the Thai total market for environmental services is growing by 20 to 30% a year. The government in Taiwan has tagged $12 billion for pollution control between 1992 and 1997.[8]

As growth in the consumption of material products has to stop, as part of the ecological strategy, business opportunities will appear in the area of services. Enhancement of quality of life will be an area of considerable value. But let us look more closely at all those businesses that produce or sell products that are environmentally destructive or highly costly. What can they do? A change in the very *field of business* will be essential for these industries if their environmental credibility is to be upheld. To give an example: Let us assume that one of the larger airlines places environment on its agenda. One step could be to replace the fleet of aircraft with new machines that use less fuel and cause less pollution. Recycled paper could be introduced in all offices and waste sorting put on the agenda. At one stroke, the airline has achieved instant environmental acceptability by these simple measures! But whether or not the aircraft replacement program is environmentally advantageous is another and more complicated question. The environmental costs of producing new and less-polluting equipment will exceed the environmental gains of less pollution and use of less fuel!

Now to the very question of field of business in our example: A socially aware and ecologically schooled management team could search for more daring changes, and ask themselves: "The business of flying involves consumption of material, creation of pollution, and heavy energy consumption. At the same time, this is our line of business, and it is useful to society. In what way does an environmentally friendly development open new business opportunities for us?" The airline could redefine its business niche from "airline" to "company for environmentally friendly communication and transport." It could take the initiative for a conference on "environment, communications, and transport." In cooperation with other airlines and supranational bodies, it could work for the development of environmentally friendly concepts. After a few years, the first "communication centers" could be established at airports or other relevant places, run by the airline. Businessmen could have their conferences with colleagues, either locally or internationally, in conference rooms equipped with audiovisual equipment. All this without recourse to flying, but still profitable for the airline. Environment campaigns could be started for "alternatives to unnecessary travelling." The company could invest in more environmentally friendly collective transport and encourage customers to consider these as alternatives to flying. The simpler actions mentioned above could be introduced concurrently.

Thus, helping an airline company into a greener niche follows the pattern of function replacement shown in Chapter 11:

1. Airborne transport of people (activity to be replaced).
2. Communication (function of the activity).
3. Communication center, environmentally friendly transport (alternative activities serving the function).

Also the replacement of another function was included:

1. Competition in airborne transport of people (activity to be replaced).
2. Maintain the position versus competitors (function of the activity).
3. Make a joint effort in the industry for the development and marketing of greener transport models (alternative activity serving the function).

Willums and Golüke, in their report for the International Environmental Bureau of the ICC (International Chamber of Commerce), say: "Perhaps the most interesting way of rethinking your services with regards to environmental impact comes when you enter a completely new business. Lufthansa, which is after all an airline, has contracted with the German railways to run two train lines: One from Frankfurt to Cologne and the other from Frankfurt to Stuttgart. The company found that in a densely populated area like Germany, and with landing slots at its hub in Frankfurt being an extremely scarce resource, it made sense to look at other transport modes to move its customers from one place to another rather than to insist on *flying* its customers to their destination.[9] Similar changes in business activity are represented, for instance, by Volkswagen, which has extended its niche from car manufacturing to traffic system development, including the utilization of public means of transport.

Ecological, ethical evaluation of products and services per se is a complicated matter. All business and industry obviously cannot change to production and sale of green technology, railway transport, and waste management. Some products, though environmentally detrimental, are at the same time perceived as such important goods that people are not ready to live without them. How should business and industry handle this? Obviously, by keeping the existing products as green as possible. Second, by developing the products in a green direction, as in our airline example. Third, by not forcing such products on the market by speculative marketing methods which generate new "needs" for unnecessary, environmentally costly products.

The businesses that first make a strong bid for the principle of *local production for local consumption for local recirculation* will be real ecological pioneers. This might be difficult, because the advantages of producing for export in low-cost countries are lost, and, to some extent, so are the advantages of mass production. Two things can be done to make it work: Cooperation in the whole industry in favor of the principle of local production for local consumption for local recycling, and activities to tie the local market to the production and the products. This may result in support from the local market for three reasons: (1) because it gives local job security, (2) because it will have the support of local environmentalist lobbyists, and (3) because it will have the support of other groups that advocate the principle of local production.

Altruistic contribution to general ecological efforts takes a high ecological consciousness. A lot of the bigger, international corporations already donate money, products, and free services to environmentalist projects. Aracruz Celulose supports several ecological programs within its area of influence: For example, the Tamar Project, "which aims to protect the reproductive cycle of five threatened species of sea turtles; the Abrolhos Marine Park—the most important ecological sanctuary in the South Atlantic; and the Marmoset Project, an attempt to reintroduce the white-faced marmoset to the company's forests."[10] The grounds for altruistic contributions are surely on different levels of moral reasoning, but some contributions carry extra value by virtue of their genuine altruistic motivation.

The businesses that practice extensive ecological changes, including some or all of the factors mentioned above, will be network builders both in business and in the community. They will gain a "holy" profile, and doors will be opened by authorities, suppliers, customers, competitors, investors, and environmentalist groups. There may be costs, but the potential gains are considerable. The direct business opportunities in the emerging niches seem endless.

BENCHMARKING BEYOND GREENERY

Business and industry will divide into four groups when it comes to ecology. The first group will be the businesses that do not care, that leave the environmental problems and any engagement for an ecologically better future to politicians and the market. They may even try to evade the law, move around to the least stringent production spots, or even lobby against environmental legislation. They will meet a tough future. They will be expelled by the green networks comprising their competitors, suppliers, retailers, consumers, authorities, and environmentalists.

The second group will consist of those that join the greening of business wave. They will make environmentally friendly adjustments in all possible areas inside their business niche, and strive to be "good citizens" of the green networks. They will contribute to sound development, mainly through simple green changes. But, for the businesses in this group, no ecological actions will be taken at the cost of profitability.

The third group will be those that march ahead, that rethink their whole business and advocate congruently their ecological ideals. They will be strong proponents of the greening of business. They will be at the forefront of the networks, even lobbying to pull the governmental regulations and policies in a green direction. They will respect ethical ecological principles in all their doings.

The fourth group will represent the radical rethinkers of all business practice, based on advanced ecological understanding. They will be ready to let traditional business opportunities go when in conflict with ecological ethics, and, as a matter of course, always place consideration for ecological values first. They will be the proponents of real ecological changes in business. They will be spokesmen for the defense of local cultures and for the principle of local production for local consumption for local recirculation. They will participate in ecological, cross-disciplinary networks that do research and contribute to real sustainability for the coming generations.

It is the joint forces of the three last groups, combined with continuous benchmarking between the businesses that belong to them, that will really contribute to an ecologically sound and sustainable future. To illustrate the importance of benchmarking, let us look shortly at, for example, Xerox: "Canon had taken a high profile on environmental issues, incorporating 'ecology' into its corporate priorities. In November 1991, Canon kicked off their Clean Earth Campaign to collect and recycle toner cartridges, relying on UPS to orchestrate the retrieval and delivery process. Canon even donated $1 per collected cartridge to the National Wildlife Federation and the Nature Conservancy.... Higher-volume copier and printer manufacturers, IBM and Eastman Kodak were competitors that Xerox also followed closely.... Benchmarking the activities of its competitors helped in the development of Xerox's environmental initiatives and was an integral part of the Leadership Through Quality initiative. But benchmarking was not limited to their direct competitors. Xerox also considered the activities of other organizations including 3M, BMW, Volkswagen, and Chemical Manufacturers Association."[11]

ECOLOGICAL CONGRUITY

"If you are in the health-care business, you can't play games with your employees' health and safety," Frances Cairncross cites Jack Mullen in Johnson & Johnson.[12] She also states that bad employers probably cannot be good environmentalists. Whether this is true or not, the perspective is of interest. The opportunities for great investments and profit at hand, through both the exploitation of the growing new business niches and the greening of the old ones, represent one side of the matter. The ecological path also implies tremendous inspiration for the ecologically aware and conscious manager of tomorrow, and a motivational force for all employees, seeing themselves as a team of ecological pioneers.

The successful managers of tomorrow will share the different ideas of team-based business, self-organizing teams, delegation of management, delayered organizations, decentralized SBUs, customer-driven R&D, service management, total quality, and strategic leadership. I believe all these to be sound contributions to comprehensive theories of business, organization, and management, and to be fully compatible with the ecological path.

Good management is profitable. Congruence between means and ends, theory and practice, personal lifestyle and message, gives stronger managerial impact. Common ecological values, policies, and goals will strengthen your company and reduce conflicts. Passionate, environmentally engaged managers are already setting the trend.[13]

SCALE YOUR COMPANY: PERFORMANCE ON
ECOLOGICAL SOUNDNESS

Law-abiding and Cost-cutting Business

If the answer to all five questions is "yes" or "irrelevant," you belong to this or the next group:

• Does your company hold a high degree of emergency preparedness?
• Do you practice safe disposal of residual waste?
• Is pollution minimized and within legal standards?
• Is amount of energy expended minimized?

• Is amount of materials expended minimized?

Plain Green Business

If the answer to the above and the following five questions is "yes" or "irrelevant," you belong to this or the next group:

• Do you hold ecology and environmental protection as a strategic focus area?
• Do you practice waste sorting?
• Do you practice product and material recycling?
• Do you practice ecological education of customers and suppliers?
• Do you practice ecological education of employees?

Ecologically Pioneering Business

If the answer to the above and the following five questions is "yes" or "irrelevant," you belong to this or the next group:

• Does your company give priority to green R&D?
• Are your working environments ecologically sound?
• Do you avoid taxation of irreplaceable raw materials as far as possible?
• Do you avoid taxation of virgin land?
• Do you avoid taxation of biodiversity?

Radical Ecological Rethinking Business

If the answer to the above and the following six questions is "yes" or "irrelevant," you belong to this group:

• Does your company buy used and recycled equipment whenever this can fill the need?
• Do you practice repairing and reusing of usable equipment?
• Do you stick to green business partners only, or educate those who are not yet green?
• Do you produce and distribute ecologically sound products and services only?
• Do you follow the principle of local production for local consumption for local recycling?
• Do you contribute altruistically to general ecological efforts?

SCALE YOURSELF: PERFORMANCE
ON ECOLOGICAL SOUNDNESS

• Do you practice the above principles in your private life? (Leave out green R&D, production and distribution, and the question of green business partners. Think of yourself or your family as the company when it comes to strategic focus area and other questions).

Appendixes

Appendix 1

Axioms of Organizational Ecology

THE SYSTEMS AXIOMS

Axiom I.1: Common Interests

Within the ecosystem, all components are kindred and interrelated. Individuals and groups within an ecosystem and within an organization are mutually dependent on each other and thereby have governing common interests.

Cooperation toward common goals should be the rule in organizations.

Axiom I.2: Self-Organizing

Ecosystems and organizations cannot be managed from the outside without high risk of erroneous prediction and instability of the system.

Self-organizing should be the aim in organizations.

Axiom I.3: Theoretical Optimums

For all ecosystems and organizations there is a theoretical optimum level of productivity, and an optimum balance between stabilizing activity and adaptive change.

Formulation of optimum, not maximum or minimum, goals and actions should be the rule in organizations.

Axiom I.4: Feedback

To adapt successfully, ecosystems and organizations are dependent on feedback. Systems that are too closed to feedback degenerate and/or die out, systems that are too open are vulnerable and lose identity.

Free flow of relevant feedback should be the rule inside organizations, and they should be characterized by an optimum degree of openness to the environment.

Axiom I.5: Diversity

Diversity is conditional for evolution, adaptation, and stability in ecosystems and in organizations. Monocultures are naturally destroyed and/ or die out.

Diversity should characterize organizations.

Axiom I.6: Conditions for Results

Optimum effects of influences, external and internal, on ecosystems or organizations are dependent on:

—Whether the element which is influenced is a core element or not
—The context
—The order in which the influences appear
—The number of links the influences pass through
—The stage of development of the system.

In all organizational change, choice of element to influence, context, order of influences, number of links, and stage of development should be taken into consideration, to prevent resistance and to attain optimum results relative to the efforts.

Axiom I.7: Function Replacement

All components in an ecosystem have a function. All behavior in an organization carries functions. If the components or the behavior are changed or removed, the more essential functions should be replaced, to maintain stability.

In all organizational change, an analysis of the functions of the elements to be changed should be performed. These should be analyzed from the first, second, and third positions, and important functions should be replaced, to prevent resistance and to reach optimum results.

THE AXIOMS OF ARCHAIC MAN

Axiom II.1: Territoriality

Humans establish and defend territories in nature and in organizations, through:

—Common contributions to governing goals

—Contrasting themselves with other groups

—Developing group symbols, rituals, and communication

—Developing common rules and beliefs

Governing common goals, values, symbols, and actions should be established to provide a common territory and identity, and a sound motivational climate in the organization.

Axiom II.2: Hierarchies

Humans establish hierarchical groups and/or communities.
An unambiguous, formal hierarchy should be established and supported to prevent hierarchy-related strife in the organization.

Axiom II.3: Man's Natural Environment

Humans, by evolution, are adapted to environments giving opportunity to:

—enjoy natural physiochemical environments

—enjoy broad variations of patterns of movement and tasks

—enjoy varied sensory exposure

—explore, and learn by experience

—obtain an overview of and meaning to their own existence

—enjoy affiliation to a group

—exist in surveyable communities and institutions

Ecologically sound working environments are physiochemically natural, provide opportunity to enjoy different tasks and patterns of movement and varied sensory exposure, opportunity to explore and to learn by experience, overview of and meaning to one's own existence, and social belonging and surveyability.

Axiom II.4: Problem Solving

Humans, by evolution, are adapted to environments favoring the taking of actions based on direct, perceivable information and simple cause-and-effect thinking. Modern environments require new problem-solving strategies that have to be learned.

Problem solving considering all mental positions, higher system levels, ecosystem patterns, and characteristics of ancient man should be applied in organizations.

Appendix 2

Problem Solving and Hierarchical Thinking

To operate in our present environment, we must be armed with tools to change and solve problems in an effective manner. Let us look deeper, now, into the world of hierarchies that we touched upon in Chapter 2. We can identify six different hierarchies of interest (Figure A2.1). To omit errors of thinking, we need to know the differences between them and the use of them. The *organizational hierarchy*, together with the *hierarchy of values* and *hierarchy of priorities*, speaks for itself. The others have broader fields of application.

Hierarchy of logical levels. Let us consider all phraseology placed on a vertical line. At the top we have general and abstract wording. As we descend, the wording becomes more and more specific. Right at the bottom we find concrete descriptions of how something looks, sounds, feels, smells, tastes. The communication's productivity depends on it being at an optimum level of precision. We may say that precisely formulated expressions are at a low logical level, while generally formulated expressions are at a high logical level. Visions, business descriptions, purposes, and intentions ought to be formulated at a high logical level, that is, generally formulated. Decisions, reports, action plans, and specific instructions ought usually to be relatively precisely defined—formulated at a low logical level.

But precise formulation of the wording may also become pedantic, and then becomes an expression of attention to minute detail, which is unproductive. It also can prevent independent and creative thinking. In some situations precise definition can cause conflict where a broader formulation would have been more suitable. However, lack of precision in communications is the most common weakness to be found in organizations. It is

Figure A2.1
Six Different Hierarchies in Problem Solving

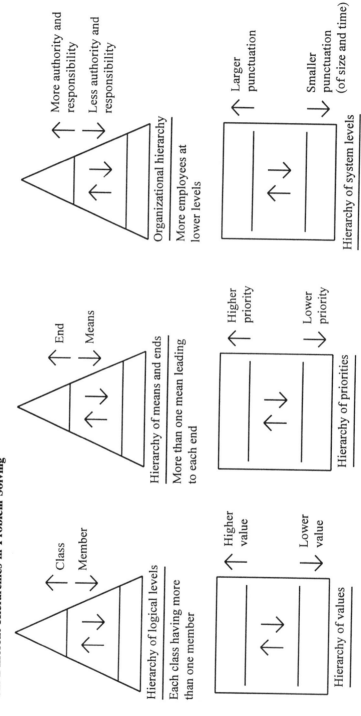

amazing to see how many misunderstandings arise from this source: A director ended a meeting with the words: "We must now make a special effort for the company in the time to come." At the end of the meeting he was asked to be more precise, what was he getting at? "Well," he said, "what I really mean is that the sales team must sell better in relation to head count." How, specifically, had he thought this could be done? "We really ought to sack one man, and the others ought to keep to the present daily performance level." He was asked who, specifically, should leave. After due consideration he came up with a name. Two other participants were then asked what they thought the director was referring to. One thought it was an early warning that the sales team was to be asked to work overtime. The other thought it was all about impending wage adjustments at the company. It was a signal, he thought, that the director would be taking a hard line.

A vision should be formulated generally at such a high level as to allow several alternative paths forward. The business description should be formulated generally at such a high level as to allow restructuring, especially in a more environmentally friendly direction, without having to modify it.

Tools for changing levels in a hierarchy of logical levels:

1. Tools for precise formulation (downward through logical levels):
   a. Ask for members of the class.
      Example: "The class of public environmental concern poses a challenge to us. What would be a member of that class?"

   "The new legislation being prepared on management of hazardous waste."

   You can also:

   b. Ask for one or more examples

   c. Ask what would be proof or evidence

   d. Ask how it would look, sound, feel

   e. Use the questioning words who, what, where, how, why, which, when

   f. Give suggestions for precise formulation.

2. Tools for general formulation (upward through logical levels):
   a. Ask which class this is a member of. Example: "Waste sorting should be considered in this firm. What class of actions would waste sorting be a member of?"

   "It belongs to the class of strategic environmental actions."

   You can also:

   b. Ask what it is an example of

   c. Ask what it is an expression of.

Hierarchy of means and ends. In order to understand a matter it is important to be able to switch between means and ends. For example, we may have witnessed a particular action that we disliked. But if we look at the intent behind the action, and thereby move up one or more levels toward the end, we may achieve a more constructive understanding of the action. We may even suggest alternative courses of action. This can be illustrated by a little history from a nonbusiness context: Prior to admission to therapy, a young man was interviewed by a psychologist about his criminal career. The psychologist systematically asked questions aimed at the intention of the behavior, moving upward from means to ends in the hierarchy. He obtained the following three general formulations: The activity gave a feeling of belonging to and respect in a group of like-minded youths. Second, it gave an experience of affinity with the father, who also had a criminal background. Finally, it provided an economic basis for material existence. The psychologist and the youth then concluded that belonging, respect, affiliation, and existence all had a positive intent. These were to be regarded as important functions in the young man's life which could not be ignored, but should be taken care of in order to maintain a personal well-being. The therapy they commenced had the following goal: To discover and try out new and better alternatives to criminal activity, in order to be able to uphold this activity's positive intent.

Tools for changing levels in a hierarchy of means and ends:

1. Tools for identifying means (downward to means):
   a. Ask for means to reach the objective.
      Example: "Our goal is to gain a reputation in the market as 'the greenest in industry.' What would be a means to reach that goal?"

   "A program for educating our suppliers in greening, and demanding results from all of them within one year."

   You can also:

   b. Suggest possible means.

2. Tools for identifying ends (upward to ends):
   a. Ask what objective this action is directed at.
      Example: "We need a thorough discussion of our environmental strategy at middle-management level. What is the objective of arranging such a discussion?"

   "To develop ownership of the strategy among our middle managers."

   You can also:

   b. Ask for the desired outcome of the action

   c. Ask for the potential gain from the action.

The application of these tools was conditional in our models for 3rd order negotiation, feedback, and problem-solving. Also, our model for function replacement relies on these tools, as shown in Chapter 11.

Hierarchy of system levels. As was shown in Chapter 2, all perception, thinking, and problem-solving necessarily imply punctuation. This insight opens the door to conscious selection of a sensible level in the hierarchy of system levels. This is how it is done:

Tools for changing levels in a hierarchy of system levels:

1. Tools for making a smaller punctuation (downward in levels):
   a. Ask what a smaller punctuation would encompass.
      Example: "Before the year 2000, total emissions of sulphur dioxide from our factories must be reduced by 64%. What would be a reasonable punctuation for us to handle at level of strategic goals?"

      "Let us look at our West European factories the next three years."

   You can also:
   b. Ask for an example of a smaller part of the system in question
   c. Ask for an example of a system which the system in question sets conditions for.

2. Tools for making a larger punctuation (upward in levels):
   a. Ask what a larger punctuation would encompass.
      Example: "We need to totally rethink the organization of our service department. What larger punctuation should be considered in this connection?"

      "I would say we start with the whole service system including customers, in light of corporate strategy."

   You can also:
   b. Ask what larger system the system in question is part of
   c. Ask which larger system sets conditions for the system in question.

When formulating goals or objectives, a check should always be made with the larger/more long-term goals of which our goals/objectives are part. If our goals/objectives contradict the goals of the larger punctuated system, they must be reconsidered.

When actions are planned, we should check if the system planning the action is in control of the essential conditions. It is essential to know which larger system sets the conditions. Overseeing this has been disastrous for a lot of well-intended improvement programs in organizations.

At the same time, actions, objectives, and goals, after checking upward, should be formulated at a reasonable low level of the hierarchy; otherwise they are difficult to identify with, and therefore lose their motivational force. A saying goes like this: "In the perspective of eternity most actions appear to be meaningless."

Appendix 3

Criteria for the Well-Formed Strategy Document

In this appendix we shall take a closer look at the main elements of a strategy document, and summarize the criteria for a well-formed strategy. The new criteria, based on environmental awareness and ecological considerations, are added.

Successful strategic planning requires various preparations. One obvious precondition is general information and necessary analyses in all areas of activity. Without this, strategic planning is mere wishful thinking. In addition, two preliminary documents are common: the SWOT analysis and the scenarios.

The SWOT analysis consists of relevant information on the here-and-now situation and on trends within all areas of activity. These are sorted, as the name indicates, in the areas of internal Strengths and Weaknesses (see Figure A3.1), and external Opportunities and Threats.

The scenarios describe the possible trends in a longer time frame, the same frame as for the vision, or even longer. Because prediction of course is uncertain, many companies prefer many parallel scenarios, implying worst case and best case. This is the most general and longitudinal basis for strategic planning (Figure A3.2). It is also highly recommendable to link benchmarking to the strategy process, as part of preparations, and as a basis for comparative follow-up.[1]

Let us now go through the criteria for each part of the complete, well-formed strategy document.

BUSINESS DESCRIPTION

Criteria for the organization's business description:

1. It should describe the field in which the organization works, that is, its products, and/or services, and market.

2. It should describe the organization's range of acceptable positions in the market.

3. It should be formulated in a sufficiently general manner so that all employees can identify themselves with it, and it should give room for varied activities. At the same time, it should be formulated with sufficient precision to enable the enterprise to have an identity, and it should provide a clear framework for the business.

4. *It should leave openings for development of products and services in an ecologically sound direction, as both the greening of the existing range and the development of new ones.*

MISSION STATEMENT

Criteria for the organization's mission statement:

1. It should describe the organization's responsibilities toward the shareholders.

2. *It should describe the organization's responsibilities toward the employees and its support to ecologically sound working conditions.*

3. It should describe the organization's responsibilities toward the customers.

4. It should describe the organization's responsibilities toward society at large.

5. *It should describe the organization's responsibilities toward the environment and an ecologically sounder future.*

VISION

Criteria for the organization's vision:

1. It should describe what the organization wishes to achieve in ideal terms in the future.

2. It should be daring and attractive (and not a little unrealistic).

3. It should not be in opposition to the prime interests or ideals of individuals or individual groups (within the organization). Ideally, it can be shared by everyone within the organization.

4. It should have both an egoistic (for the enterprise itself) and an altruistic (for the larger society) aspect.

5. The vision should have a time aspect that is suited to the organization.

6. *The vision should describe the firm's contribution to an ecologically sounder future.*

Figure A3.1
Matrix of Strategic Strengths and Weaknesses, Including Ecology/Environment as a Possible Focus

	Finance	Economy	Marketing	Sales	Production	Products & Services	Research & Development	Organization	General Picture
Volume									
Quality									
Productivity									
Human Resources									
Technology									
Ecology/ Environment									

The elements of the vertical column to the left label different aspects of the elements in the horizontal upper row.

Fill in with W, S, N or X, where:

W = Weakness ("Needs to be improved in the upcoming strategy period")

S = Strength ("Strong enough for the upcoming strategy period")

N = Neutral ("Strong enough, but keep an eye on in the upcoming strategy period")

X = Irrelevant ("Irrelevant for the upcoming strategy period")

Figure A3.2
The Process of Formulating a Strategy

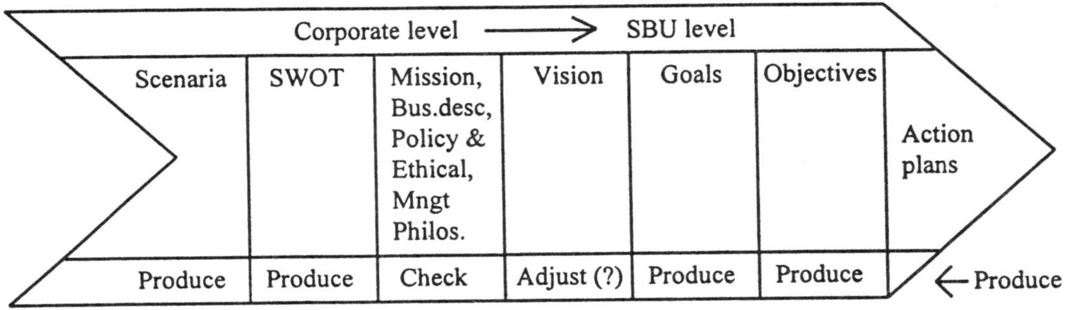

	Corporate level → SBU level					
Scenaria	SWOT	Mission, Bus.desc, Policy & Ethical, Mngt Philos.	Vision	Goals	Objectives	Action plans
Produce	Produce	Check	Adjust (?)	Produce	Produce	← Produce

MAIN GOALS

Main goals are the organization's milestones that it sets out to reach. These should be formulated for a set of *focus areas*. These focus areas are chosen from the complete set of areas of activity. A simple overview of all areas was shown in Figure 1.1.

Criteria for the organization's main goals:

1. They should describe what the organization wishes to achieve.
2. The goals should be formulated in a way that enables them to be quantified, providing the basis for knowing whether they have been achieved.
3. Sound main goals should be realistic ones. It should be possible to derive objectives and actions from them.
4. The timing aspect surrounding the main goals should equate to the value-creating cycle of the particular field of activity.
5. Main goals should be in accord with the business description, the mission statement, and the vision, as well as the conditions imposed on the business by the board of directors or a corresponding body.
6. *At least one main goal should be formulated inside the focus area of ecology.*

POLICY AND ETHICAL GUIDELINES

The organization's policy and ethical guidelines reflect its basic values. The policy and ethical guidelines can remain unchanged throughout its whole existence. This creates trust and reliability among employees as well as in the market.

Criteria for the organization's policy and ethical guidelines:

1. They should describe the organization's rules of conduct with respect to the relationship between management and other employees and between peers.
2. *They should describe the organization's rules of conduct in relation to the environment, and the organization's customers, competitors, suppliers, the industry, and society at large.*
3. *They should describe the enterprise's general ethical guidelines and its ecological ethical guidelines in special.*

Contrary to what I have indicated as the desired development, the trend is toward one worldwide marketplace. This means that the political and social control of business is declining. At the same time, the threats to the environment caused by modern technology's production are growing. This implies that, more than ever, there is strong need for internal control and strong internal ethics in the corporations.

MANAGEMENT PHILOSOPHY

In general, the management philosophy also has high durability. In times of dramatic and quick changes in the market, a management philosophy is more important than ever. Well-harmonized and loyal management teams are a precondition for success, one of the central building bricks being a management philosophy.

Criteria for the organization's management philosophy:

1. It should be in accordance with the organization's policy and ethical guidelines.
2. It should describe a common theoretical framework for leadership.
3. It should be formulated at a medium logical level, so that it gives a basis for a common managerial approach, while at the same time leaving room for individual managerial styles.
4. It should give guidelines for managerial behavior toward employees, peers, superiors, customers, suppliers, and competitors.
5. *A modern, ecological worldview should be reflected in the management philosophy.*

Appendix 4

A Critique of the Strategy of Global Economic Growth

I do not think that there are serious disagreements as to the superior values of ecology as I have summarized them in this book: The intrinsic value of nature, mankind, and human happiness. The norms derived from these values also should gather general agreement. One of the norms, however, is highly controversial: 3b. "Communities should be based mainly on self-sufficiency!" A discussion of this norm is implicit in the following.

There seem to be two main strategies for an ecologically sound future for mankind. The first one, which I have advocated, I have named the "ecological path." The second strategy we can call the "path of global economic growth."

THE PATH OF GLOBAL ECONOMIC GROWTH

This strategy has very influential supporters. The World Commission on Environment and Development of 1987 gave much of the principal ballast. The basic idea is to fulfill the present needs of mankind in a way that does not compromise the needs of future generations.[1] One influential advocate for this view is the International Chamber of Commerce (ICC). As it declares in its principles for Environmental Management: "Economical growth provides the conditions in which protection of the environment can best be achieved, and environmental protection, in balance with other human goals, is necessary to achieve growth that is sustainable. In turn, versatile, dynamic, responsive and profitable businesses are required as the driving force for sustainable economic development and for providing managerial, technical and financial resources to contribute to the resolution of environmental challenges. Market economies, characterized by entrepreneurial initiatives, are essential to achieving this."[2]

It also declares: "Open trade is a key requirement for sustainable development. The progressive liberalization of international trade and investment has stimulated global economical growth, including growth in developing countries that have moved towards market-oriented policies." And: "The problem at hand is not only one of environment—it is also one about exploding population and poverty, and deteriorating health. In many developing nations poverty, population growth and environmental damage are very closely related. Protection of the local as well as global environment must therefore be integral to the development process everywhere because the world is becoming increasingly interdependent."[3]

Let us take as our starting point the intrinsic value of nature, mankind, and human happiness. The above quotation then adds to our values concerning mankind and human beings the values of defeating poverty and increasing health. They fit well, since they may be seen as special cases of the intrinsic value of human happiness. The idea is that business should contribute to sustainable development, defeat of poverty, and better health among people of the earth. The strategy of global economic growth follows this logic: Global economic growth based on increased world trade and one free-world market will promote work sharing between countries, thus exploiting the competitive advantages of different regions and improving global productivity. It will give the developing countries access to capital and technology, thus meeting the preconditions for economic growth in these countries. This represents a win-win situation between the rich and the poor world, where the rich world will gain new opportunities for further growth and enhanced economical and technological power to defeat environmental problems in the rich world. This will stimulate further technological advancements in the areas of green technology and high-yielding agricultural technology. This again will feed back to the developing countries as improved methods in industry and agriculture, defeating environmental problems and poverty. When poverty is defeated illiteracy can be defeated and health improvement programs can be financed and implemented. The defeat of illiteracy also means that the population will take into use contraceptives, and this will represent a victory over the problem of overpopulation. When poverty and overpopulation are eradicated, environmental problems caused by the panic behavior of people in this situation also will be solved.

Global economic growth by this solves the environmental problems in both the developing and the developed countries, and meets the preconditions for eradicating illiteracy, poverty, health problems and overpopulation. Let us evaluate this strategy.

Improved global productivity. There is no such thing as global productivity. There is no reciprocity between the rich and the poor world. The global economic growth paradigm leads to more poverty for most people in the third and fourth worlds. The second, third and fourth worlds cannot compete with the first world. It's like letting a one-year-old and an adult athlete into Forum Romanum, giving them each a sword and instructing them to fight a fair match. As constant losers in this race, developing countries lose everything: Instead of growing richer they grow poorer and poorer. It is a matter of fact that since the early 1980s, the developing countries have fallen ever deeper into poverty, while the first world has become richer. Instead of experiencing positive cultural development, poor countries might as well experience cultural collapse, which we know represents a threat to common health and well-being. Instead of increased happiness there might as well be increased desperation and depression.

Transport is a fundamental source of resource spending, energy use, and pollution. By this world trade exerts direct and heavy stress on the environment. Both the rich world and the poor world lose by this strategy. Both of them lose hold of the regulatory mechanisms that are characteristic of a free market with barriers. Bad methods of production, bad ethics, and bad products are less probable when your friends and neighbors are your market. Overproduction and carelessness about the environment are less probable in such a situation. When your production unit is on one side of the globe and your market is on the other side, the feedback loop between the producer and his market is broken. Only the very ethically developed business will stay ethical in a situation where there are no possibilities for market sanctions. Free international trade and competition often lead to lowered quality of life and living standards in the developing world, bad environmental effects, cultural collapse, and decreased happiness, the opposite of what was intended.

Capital and technology to the developing countries. Introduction of capital and technology can cause positive or negative effects in developing countries. There is no general evidence that it leads to higher living standards and generally better conditions for the people. In the rich world there has been a slow coevolution of technological, economic, political, social, psychological, and ethical factors. This has been preconditional for the rich world to handle the modern times. And even then tremendous problems have followed in the wake of economic and technological developments.

Power to defeat environmental problems in the rich world. Economic growth to defeat environmental problems is like voluntarily spreading a disease with the intention of selling a cure for it afterward! The main road to victory over environmental problems lies in negative economic growth and lowered material production and consumption in the rich world.[4]

Improved methods in industry and agriculture defeating environmental problems and poverty in the developing countries. New methods in agriculture based on HYV (High Yielding Variety) and a general mechanizing is ecologically hazardous and socially risky. There is no substantial reason to say that modernizing agriculture and industry is a good means to defeat environmental problems and poverty in developing countries. A lot of other factors must be present for this to work satisfactorily. Industrializing also will cause new environmental problems.

Defeating illiteracy. Illiteracy can be defeated, and has been defeated very effectively without global economic growth. In fact, illiteracy in many places is a *consequence* of cultural breakdown in developing countries that have been colonized or in other ways exploited by the first world. Historically, we know that very poor countries have been able to eradicate illiteracy.

Health improvement programs. Modern medicine is a complicated matter for evaluation. It is not a matter of course that it is good or better than local methods in the developing countries. Like all our modern technology, it is part of a broad cultural evolution. To implement this mechanically in any culture as a "good" is to show ignorance for local cultures. Both international aid programs and business investors in the health industry should bear this in mind. Historically, countries have succeeded with health improvement programs independently of global economic growth.

Contraceptives against overpopulation. Contraceptives exist in most traditional cultures, and different methods have always existed for preventing overpopulation. These cultures must be given the opportunity to refind their own contraceptive methods, their own population-regulating mechanisms, and the system's own means of regulation. At the same time, the first world should of course be ready to support the countries that are ready to use modern contraceptives. This is an important task for the international society.

There also is reason to question the causal link between poverty and illiteracy on the one hand, and population growth on the other. In many developing countries birth rates are now falling, although living standards and degree of illiteracy remain unchanged. Family planning programs may be one of the factors causing this.[5]

THE BASIC MISTAKES OF GLOBAL ECONOMIC GROWTH

To further understand the deep misconceptions leading up to this strategy, we should look again at the concepts of mental positions and punctuation. Industrial man, like everyone else, does his best to keep his second, third, and fourth position evaluations objective. Highly valued tools for him are science and logic. But science and logic do not provide answers about values and ethics, other people's feelings, and one's own subjectivity. A hidden premise in the strategy of global economic growth is that "it is better for the world's different cultures that they develop to become like us. They should have our technology, our democracy, and our market economy." But this obviously is a first position point of view. Ranking of cultures, races, or individuals is dangerous. It too easily leads to colonialism, imperialism, racism, and oppression. The fact of its being well-intentioned is of little consolation to its victims.

The next basis for this mistaken strategy is the confusion of living standard with quality of life. As we saw, there is no significant correlation between the two. And subjective happiness has different contents and values on a Caribbean island, in Hollywood, in Lapland, and in Tokyo. The mistake obviously is linked to a general confusion of technological systems with systems of living organisms. In technology, accurate prediction and management are possible. But living systems are self-organizing. All cultures must be given a chance to develop in their own way. What is good for the United States is not necessarily good for Gambia or Cameroon.

Let us look at the problem with still another set of concepts, a new set of "invisible patterns." Sometimes the way we go about solving problems brings us deeper into the morass. The concept that "the solution is the problem" is introduced by human systems theory pioneer Paul Watzlawick.[6] He describes four categories of problem creation, all of which are of relevance to this discussion.

The first category is the situation where something that is not a problem is "solved," thereby causing problems, or "repairing the unbroken." A sensitive and well-fed mother who worries about her teenage daughter being underweight could serve as an example. She has read about Anorexia Nervosa and decides to put her daughter on a diet. She pushes her to eat more, makes delicious meals, and organizes family life to make meals cozy and attractive. Her daughter, originally a slim and healthy teenage girl, rejects this project. The best way is by not eating. Her counterstrategy to safeguard identity and autonomy then leads her into Anorexia Nervosa. The third and fourth world people have been exposed to this problem-creation category again and again. The ideas of civilizing the "uncivilized" or developing the "less developed" are solutions to nonproblems which generate problems.

The next category is found where an attempt is made to solve a problem with more of an ineffective medicine, "more of the same," causing new problems. The wrong antibiotic does not cure an illness even in large amounts. But the side effects may cause new physical problems. A child who does not listen to the parents' good advice listens less and less the more the advice is given. At one point of time, the solution for the child will be to do the opposite of the advice.

The problems of poverty in the third and fourth world are largely problems of this category. The wrong medicine is a global market and economic growth, where the right medicine would be to support autonomous development and self-sufficiency in a long-term perspective. The state of affairs in the second world, the ex-communist regimes, also were examples of this category. Low efficiency and corruption were products of the bureaucratic communist state model, and "more of the same" led to even lower efficiency and more corruption.

A third category is where an attempt is made to produce a desirable development, which is spontaneous by nature, by direct pressure or intervention. As a parent you cannot teach your children everything directly. The ability to enjoy literature is learned by modelling and experience, not by the order "enjoy literature!" A husband who demands of his wife "love me!" is bound to lose out. Harmonious cultural development and balance don't come with orders like "develop democracy and market economy!" This is relevant both in situations where the order comes from outside and where it comes from representatives of this position inside the culture. Mechanistic thinking, confusing the universe of machines with the universe of living organisms, causes such problems in all four worlds.

A difficulty that is denied, and thereby not given adequate solutions, may develop into a manifest problem. This constitutes the fourth category of problem creation. A teenage girl who starts excessive slimming in fact *may* represent a first stage of Anorexia Nervosa. Not taking action to help her change her behavior may make the problem worse. This is not the most typical category in our context here. However, the denial of the bad consequences of the global economic growth paradigm may fit.

I would like to add a fifth category having to do with impatience or wrong punctuation of time. I think of a situation where the right medicine is prescribed, but healing takes time. When no signs of healing appear immediately, or the problem gets even worse, the medicine is dropped, and new, wrong medicines are introduced. This is especially relevant in situations where "things grow worse before they grow better." Decision makers who do not keep an ice-cold head too easily fall victim to this category of problem creation. For example, when new routines are introduced in an organization, usually some difficulties will follow. Taking these difficulties to be proof of the new routines being wrong is a main fault. As so many parents have experienced, setting limitations for children for the sake of sound discipline leads to a *worsening* of the relationship at first. But in the long run, the relationship is strengthened.

Industrial man too often has brief perspectives for his actions. But cultural self-organizing takes time, the solutions of the international ecological and human problems necessarily take time. All four worlds suffer by the short perspectives of time that ride industrial man.

A situation where the immediate good results of an action lead to the automatic continued use of it could be mentioned as a sixth category. The drink that eases your nerves today makes you an alcoholic next year. This perhaps is the most typical category of problem creation generally leading to ecological problems. The immediate good results of biotechnology in laboratories or other strictly limited conditions should not lead automatically to expanded use of it. In fact, the whole idea of economic growth basically fits this category. All four worlds suffer from this misconception.

Most of these categories describe problems caused by doing; only one shows problems caused by not doing (Table A4.1). I see this as an accurate description of the situation. Most ecological problems, and problems of worldwide human suffering, are caused by industrial man's *doing*, rarely by his *not doing*.

Table A4.1
Six Different Patterns of Problem Creation

Six categories of problem formation	
Category 1:	Fixing the unbroken
Category 2:	More of the same interventions that does not work
Category 3:	Planning and steering the unpredictable and spontaneous
Category 4:	Denying the problem and not intervening
Category 5:	Stopping sound interventions as improvement takes time - because things get worse (before they get better)
Category 6:	More of the same interventions that does work, in greater amounts leading to "intoxication"

Notes

1. THE NEW MEGATREND

1. Numbers from Commerzbank report, *The Economist* (October 23, 1993), p. 74.

2. The biggest being the French company Générale des Eaux. Source for this information is *The Economist*, May 29, 1993.

3. Willums and Golüke 1992.

4. Ibid.

5. These numbers are taken from Ottman 1993. The book contains a lot of relevant and valid information on the greening of business.

6. Numbers from tables covering seven major organizations in the United States and England, in Cairncross 1991.

7. Quoted from "Xerox: Design for the Environment," case study at Harvard Business School, prepared by Fiona E. S. Murray. Quoted with permission from Xerox Corporation.

8. See, for example, Koechlin and Müller 1992; Elkington 1989; Carson and Moulden 1991; Ottman 1993.

9. Information taken from Naisbitt and Aburdene 1990.

10. Quote from Naisbitt 1994, p. 104.

11. Numbers from *The Economist: Pocket World in Figures,* 1994. London: The Economist Books Ltd.

12. John Naisbitt's idea of the global paradox: A future of one world, thanks to effective telecommunications emerging parallel to a further division of nations and countries into smaller units. See Naisbitt 1994.

13. Local production for local consumption for local recirculation is an ecological principle to be elaborated on in Chapters 3 and 19.

14. Quote from Kennedy 1993, p. 159.

15. Quote from Drucker 1992, p. 259.

16. Ibid.
17. Quoted from Naisbitt 1994, p. 40.
18. See, for example, Cairncross 1991.
19. Ibid., p. 222.
20. Quoted from Haskins 1990, p. 29.

2. CONCEPTS OF HELP

1. See Bateson 1972.
2. The concept of filters is taken from DeLozier and Grinder 1987.
3. The concepts of first, second, and third position are also used by DeLozier and Grinder (see DeLozier and Grinder 1987).
4. I owe this use of the concept to John Grinder.
5. The three categories mainly follow Gregory Bateson's criteria for different types of learning (see Bateson 1972, pp. 279–308).

3. A BRIEF LESSON ON ECOSYSTEMS

1. Quoted from Georgescu-Roegen 1972, p. 17.
2. Taken from Delin 1985.
3. It takes a truly cross-disciplinary perspective to evaluate the total effects of the green revolution. Statistics showing growth only in gross production of, for example, rice and wheat are misleading. A well-documented critique of this "progress" is found in Shiva 1988. A discussion of alternatives is found, for example, in Bray 1994.
4. A thorough analysis of cooperation, harmony, and purpose in nature is found in, for example, Augros and Stanciu 1988.
5. The concepts of positive and negative feedback have caused many misunderstandings. They should not be confused with the everyday use, where negative feedback implies a reprimand and positive feedback implies praise. The scientific, not the everyday meaning is intended all through this book when the phrases are used.
6. The examples of European rabbits in Australia and wood pigeons in England are taken from Krebs 1988.
7. Examples from Augros and Stanciu 1988.

4. ORGANIZATIONAL ECOLOGY

1. A thorough account of this view is found in Hannan 1989.
2. Gareth Morgan has made a popular overview of different metaphors used to understand organizations at different times. See Morgan 1986.
3. The concept stems from the title of Dawkins 1976.
4. See, for example, Augros and Stanciu 1988.

5. COMMON INTERESTS AND CONFLICT SOLVING

1. See Goldsmith 1992.
2. This is a popular slogan among environmentalists, formulated by the Norwegian ecosopher Arne Naess (see Naess and Rothenberg 1989).

6. SELF-ORGANIZING

1. Quoted from Drucker 1990, pp. 98–99.

2. A presentation is given in Warnecke 1993.

3. By the first world we refer to the highly industrialized world, except the former Soviet Union and East European countries, which make up the second world. By the third world we refer to the developing countries, except original cultures like indian tribes around Amazonas, aborigines in Australia, Maoris in New Zealand, and Laps in the arctic areas, which make up the fourth world.

4. The numbers and the ideas are presented in Krugman 1994.

8. FEEDBACK AND OPENNESS

1. Quoted from Drucker 1990, p. 96.

12. TERRITORIES

1. Konrad Lorenz, among others, contributed to the field of ethology with his famous work "On Aggression" (see Lorenz 1963).

2. This is based on subjective experience. We are ignorant of any systematic scoring of communication in this category of settings by criteria of territoriality. This should be a mature field for further research.

3. This experiment is described in Lepper et al. 1973.

4. Double blind testing of various medicines and therapies strongly confirms that in many instances, the placebo effect is even stronger than the medical influence. See, for example, Frank 1974.

5. See, for example, Schein 1980 for further readings on this subject.

6. The formulation of the problem and phrasing is taken from Garrett Hardin 1968.

7. See, for example, Sherif 1958, which gives an illustrative, experimental example of the principle. It constitutes a social-psychological classic in the field.

14. ECOLOGICALLY SOUND WORKING ENVIRONMENTS

1. According to surveys administered by F.J. Langdon, referred in Ornstein 1990.

2. Numbers according to Newsweek, Vol CXX, no. 23, December 7, 1992.

3. The expression is taken from Tinbergen 1976.

4. Quoted from Ornstein and Ehrlich 1989, p. 62.

15. THINKING AND PROBLEM SOLVING

1. Ornstein and Ehrlich 1989.

2. This anecdote, and a lot more, are found in Ricks 1993.

16. STRATEGY: FORMALITY OR REALITY

1. See Kotter and Heskett 1992.

2. See, for example, Kotter and Heskett 1992, and Peters and Waterman 1984.

19. ECOLOGICAL VALUES

1. See, for example, Tinbergen 1976.

2. See documentation for this in World Commission on Environment and Development 1987; Brown yearly editions; Union of Concerned Scientists 1992.

3. See Ornstein and Ehrlich 1989, p. 7–8.

4. Marc Luyckx, in The Forward Studies Unit of Commision des Communautés Européennes, quoted from Luyckx 1993, p. 47.

5. Quoted here are three out of eight statements in Naess 1988, p. 130.

6. Ibid., p. 129.

7. Quoted from Skolimowski 1992, p. 214.

8. A thorough documentation can be found in Diener 1984.

9. Quoted by Herman E. Daly, senior economist in the World Bank, in Daly 1993.

10. Quoted from Naess and Rothenberg 1989, p. 87.

11. See Schumacher 1973.

20. BUSINESS ETHICS IN THE AGE OF ECOLOGY

1. According to *The Economist*, September 3, 1994, p. 76–77.

2. Quoted from Ekins 1992, p. 93.

3. These three levels of moral reasoning are proposed by Lawrence Kohlberg. He also differentiates between two stages within each level. For the sake of simplicity, this is not detailed here. According to Kohlberg, none of the stages or levels is meant to be superior to others. He simply sees this as a line of development. For more detail and discussion, see Lerner 1976.

4. Norman Bowie in the essay *Morality, Money and Motor Cars*, quoted from Hoffman et al. 1990, p. 89.

5. Quoted from Koechlin and Müller 1992, pp. 94–95.

6. Quoted from International Chamber of Commerce. See Selected Bibliography.

21. GREEN, ETHICAL, AND PROFITABLE

1. See *Fortune*, no. 15, July 26, 1993, pp. 104–111.

2. Quoted with permission from British Gas Environmental Review 1992.

3. Quoted from Monsanto Backgrounder brochure, with permission from Monsanto Company.

4. Quoted from official advertising brochure from Canon Europe.

5. Quote and information from Willums and Golüke 1992, p. 211.

6. Ibid., p. 214.

7. Quoted from "Xerox Corporation and the Environment" brochure, with permission from Xerox Corporation.

8. According to *The Economist*, August 20, 1994, pp. 53–54.

9. Quoted from Willums and Golüke 1992, p. 149.

10. Information and quote from "Corporate Profile," Aracruz Celulose, quoted with permission.

11. Quoted from case study at Harvard Business School, prepared by Fiona E. S. Murray, with permission from Xerox Corporation.

12. In Cairncross 1991, p. 225.

13. For more details about going green, see, for instance, Sadgrove 1992 and Westerman 1993 for supervision on "how to"; and Elkington 1989 and Willums and Golüke 1992 for good examples on how to profit.

APPENDIX 3

1. See, for example, Watson 1993.

APPENDIX 4

1. See World Commission on Environment and Development 1987.

2. Quoted from leaflet from ICC, International Chamber of Commerce, Publication 210/356 A.

3. These quotes are from Willums and Golüke 1992, p. 16–18.

4. See specifically Meadows, Meadows and Randers 1991. For further discussions, see also Brown yearly editions; Naess and Rothenberg 1989; and Ehrlich and Ehrlich 1991.

5. See Robey, Rutstein and Morris 1993.

6. This concept and the following categories of problem creation are described in Watzlawick et al. 1974.

Selected Bibliography

Augros, Robert, and Stanciu, George. 1988. *The New Biology. Discovering the Wisdom in Nature*. Boston and London: The New Science Library Shambala.

Bandler, Richard, and Grinder, John. 1982. *Reframing. Neuro-Linguistic Programming and the Transformation of Meaning*. Moab, Utah: Real People Press.

Bateson, Gregory. 1972. *Steps to an Ecology of Mind*. New York: Ballantine Books.

———. 1979. *Mind and Nature: A Necessary Unit*. New York: Dutton.

Bjoernson, Bjoernstjerne. 1914. *Collected Works*, vol. 10. Kristiania, Norway: Gyldendal.

Bolman, Lee G., and Deal, Terrence E. 1991. *Reframing Organizations. Artistry, Choice and Leadership*. San Francisco: Jossey-Bass.

Bray, Francesca. 1994. "Agriculture for Developing Nations." *Scientific American* 271, no. 1: 18–25.

Brown, Lester R. *State of the World*. Washington, D.C.: Worldwatch Institute, yearly edition.

Cairncross, Frances. 1991. *Costing the Earth*. London: Business Books Ltd.

Carson, Patrick, and Moulden, Julia. 1991. *Green Is Gold*. Toronto: HarperCollins.

Daly, Herman E. 1993. "The Perils of Free Trade." *Scientific American* 269, no. 5 (November): 24-29.

Dawkins, Richard. 1976. *The Selfish Gene*. Oxford University Press.

Delin, Staffan. 1985. *Nature's Technology and Man's* (Naturens teknik och människans). Stockholm: LT Publishers. (Swedish edition)

DeLozier, Judith, and Grinder, John. 1987. *Turtles all the Way Down. Prerequisites to Personal Genius*. Bonny Doon: Grinder, DeLozier and Associates.

Diener, Ed. 1984. "Subjective Well-Being." *Psychological Bulletin* 95, no. 3: 542–575.

Drucker, Peter F. 1990. "The Emerging Theory of Manufacturing." *Harvard Business Review* (May-June): 94–102.

————. 1992. *Managing for the Future. The 1990s and Beyond.* Oxford: Butterworth-Heinemann Ltd.

The Economist: Pocket World in Figures. 1994. London: The Economist Books Ltd.

Ehrlich, Paul R., and Ehrlich, Anne H. 1991. *Healing the Planet. Strategies for Resolving the Environmental Crisis.* New York: Addison-Wesley.

Ekins, Paul. 1992. *Wealth Beyond Measure. An Atlas of New Economics.* London: Gaya Books Ltd.

Elkington, John. 1989. *The Green Capitalists.* London: Victor Gollancz Ltd.

Elkington, John, Knight, Peter, and Hailes, Julia. 1991. *The Green Business Guide.* London: Victor Gollancz Ltd.

Fisher, Roger, and Ury, William. 1981. *Getting to YES. Negotiating Agreement Without Giving In.* London: Arrow Books.

Frank, Jerome D. 1974. *Persuasion and Healing. A Comparative Study of Psychotherapy.* New York: Schocken Books.

Georgescu-Roegen, Nicholas. 1972. "Economics and Entropy." *Ecologist* 2, no. 7: 13–18.

Gibran, Kahlil. 1980. *The Prophet.* Oslo: Gyldendal.

Glassersfeld, Ernst von. 1984. "An Introduction to Radical Constructivism." In Watzlawick, Paul (ed.), *The Invented Reality.* New York: W.W. Norton.

Goldsmith, Edward. 1973. "Adam and Eve Revisited." *Ecologist* 3, no. 9 (September).

————. 1992. *The Way. An Ecological World-View.* London: Rider.

Handscombe, Richard, and Norman, Philip. 1993. *Strategic Leadership. Managing the Missing Links.* London: McGraw-Hill.

Hannan, Michael T., and Freeman, John. 1989. *Organizational Ecology.* Cambridge: Harvard University Press.

Hansen, Jon Lund et al. 1993. *Broad Ecology. A Cross-Disciplinary Challenge.* Oslo: Cappelen. (Norwegian edition)

Hardin, Garrett. 1968. "The Tragedy of the Commons." *Science* 162: 1243-1248.

Haskins, Mike S. (ed.). 1990. *The Greening of European Business.* Conference Report, Munich Marriott Hotel, Germany, October 4–5.

Hoffman, W. M., Frederick, R., and Petry, E. S., Jr. (eds.). 1990. *Business, Ethics, and the Environment. The Public Policy Debate.* Westport, Conn.: Quorum Books.

International Chamber of Commerce (ICC). "The Business Charter for Sustainable Development. Principles for Environmental Management." Brochure, Publication 210/356 A.

Jansson, Tove. 1961. *The Exploits of Moominpappa.* Oslo: Aschehoug.

Kennedy, Paul. 1993. *Preparing for the Twenty-First Century.* London: Fontana Press.

Koechlin, Dominik, and Müller, Kaspar. 1992. *Green Business Opportunities. The Profit Potential.* London: Pitman Publishing.

Kotter, John P., and Heskett, James L. 1992. *Corporate Culture and Performance.* New York: The Free Press.

Krebs, Charles J. 1988. *The Message of Ecology.* New York: Harper & Row.

Krugman, Paul. 1994. "Competitiveness: Does It Matter?" *Fortune*, no. 5 (March 7): 71–74.

Lepper, M. R., Green, P., and Nisbett, R. E. 1973. "Undermining Children's Intrinsic Interests with Extrinsic Rewards. A Test of the Overjustification Hypothesis." *Journal of Personality and Social Psychology* 28: 129–137.

Lerner, Richard M. 1976. *Concepts and Theories of Human Development*. Reading, Mass.: Addison-Wesley.

Lorenz, Konrad. 1963. *Das Sogenannte böse. Zur naturgeschichte der aggression*. Wien: Borotha-Schoeler Verlag.

———. 1968. *On Aggression*. Oslo: Cappelen. (Norwegian edition)

Luyckx, Marc. 1993. Cultural Change and Ethical Responsibilities of the Scientist." *Cybernetics and Human Knowing* 2, no. 2.

Malmberg, Torsten. 1980. *Human Territoriality*. Hague: Mouton Publishers.

Marcus, Aage. 1965. *The Blue Dragon*. Oslo: Gyldendal.

Maynard, Herman B., Jr., and Mehrtens, Susan E. 1993. *The Fourth Wave. Business in the 21st Century*. San Francisco: Berrett-Koehler Publishers.

Meadows, Donella H., Meadows, Dennis L., and Randers, Foergen. 1991. *Beyond the Limits. Confronting Global Collapse. Envisioning a Sustainable Future*. Post Mills, Vt.: Chelsea Green Publishing Co.

Merton, Robert K. 1948. "The Self-Fulfilling Prophecy." *Antioch Review*, no. 8: 193–210.

Morgan, Gareth. 1986. *Images of Organizations*. New York: Sage Publications.

Morris, Desmond. 1968. *The Naked Ape*. Oslo: Gyldendal.

Myers, Norman. 1985. *The GAIA Atlas of Planet Management for Today's Caretakers of Tomorrow's World*. London: Gaia Books Ltd.

Naess, Arne. 1988. "Deep Ecology and Ultimate Premises." *The Ecologist* 18, nos. 4/5: 128–131.

Naess, Arne, and Rothenberg, David. 1989. *Ecology, Community and Lifestyle. Outline of an Ecosophy*. New York: Cambridge University Press.

Naisbitt, John, and Aburdene, Patricia. 1990. *Megatrends 2000*. New York: William Morrow.

Naisbitt, John. 1994. *Global Paradox*. London: Nicholas Brealey Publishing.

Odum, Eugene P. 1983. *Basic Ecology*. Philadelphia: Saunders College Publishing.

Ornstein, Robert, and Ehrlich, Paul. 1989. *New World New Mind. Moving Towards Conscious Evolution*. New York: Touchstone.

Ornstein, Suzyn. 1990. "Linking Environmental and Industrial/Organizational Psychology." In Cooper, Cary L., and Robertson, Ivan T., *International Review of Industrial and Organizational Psychology*, vol. 5. New York: John Wiley & Sons.

Ottman, Jacquelyn A. 1993. *Green Marketing. Challenges & Opportunities for the New Marketing Age*. Lincolnwood, Ill.: NTC Business Books.

Palazzoli, M. S. et al. 1981. *The Hidden Games of Organizations*. New York: Pantheon Books.

Peters, Thomas J., and Waterman, Robert H. 1984. *In Search of Excellence*. New York: Harper & Row.

Reich, Robert B. 1991. *The Work of Nations. Preparing Ourselves for 21st Century Capitalism*. London, New York, Tokyo, Singapore, Toronto: Simon & Schuster.

Ricks, David A. 1993. *Blunders in International Business*. Cambridge: Blackwell Publishers.

Robey, B., Rutstein, S. O., and Morris, L. 1993. "The Fertility Decline in Developing Countries." *Scientific American* 269, no. 6: 30–37.

Rosen, Sidney. 1982. *My Voice Will Go With You. The Teaching Tales of Milton H. Erickson, M.D.* New York: W.W. Norton.

Sadgrove, Kit. 1992. *The Green Manager's Handbook.* Aldershot, England: Gower Publishing.

Schein, Edgar H. 1980. *Organizational Psychology.* New York: Prentice-Hall.

Schmidheiny, Stephan. 1992. *Changing Course. A Global Business Perspective on Development and the Environment.* Cambridge and London: Massachusetts Institute of Technology.

Schumacher, E. F. 1973. *Small Is Beautiful. A Study of Economics as if People Mattered.* London: Blond & Briggs Ltd.

Senge, Peter M. 1992. *The Fifth Discipline.* London: Century Business Books.

Sherif, Muzafer. 1958. "Superordinate Goals in the Reduction of Intergroup Conflict." *American Journal of Sociology* 63.

Shiva, Vandana. 1988. *Staying Alive.* England: Zed Press.

Skolimowski, Henryk. 1992. *Living Philosophy. Eco-Philosophy as a Tree of Life.* London: Arkana.

"A Survey of Waste and the Environment." 1993. *The Economist,* May 29.

Tinbergen, Niko. 1976. "Functional Ethology and the Human Sciences." In Hollander, Edwin P., and Hunt, Raymond G., *Current Perspectives in Social Psychology.* London and Toronto: Oxford University Press.

Toffler, Arnold. 1990. *Power Shift. Knowledge, Wealth and Violence at the Edge of the 21st Century.* New York: Bantam Books.

Tuleja, Tad. 1988. *Beyond the Bottom Line.* Stockholm: Svenska Dagbladet.

Union of Concerned Scientists. 1992. "World Scientists' Warning to Humanity." Brochure.

Vaitilingham, Romesh (ed.). 1993. *Industrial Initiatives for Environmental Conservation.* London: Pitman Publishing.

Warnecke, Hans-Jürgen. 1993. *The Fractal Company. A Revolution in Corporate Culture.* Berlin: Springer-Verlag.

Watson, Gregory H. 1993. *Strategic Benchmarking. How to Rate Your Company's Performance Against the World's Best.* New York: John Wiley & Sons.

Watzlawick, P., Weakland, J., and Fisch, R. 1974. *Change: Principles of Problem Formation and Problem Resolution.* New York: W.W. Norton.

Watzlawick, Paul. 1977. *How Real Is Real?* New York: Vintage Books.

———. 1988. *Ultra-Solutions or How to Fail Most Successfully.* New York: W.W. Norton.

Westerman, Martin D. 1993. *The Business Environmental Handbook.* Grants Pass, Ore.: The Oasis Press.

Wilden, Anthony. 1987. *The Rules Are No Game. The Strategy of Communication.* Sweden: Korgen, 1990.

Willums, Jan-Olaf, and Golüke, Ulrich. 1992. *From Ideas to Action. Business and Sustainable Development. The ICC Report on The Greening of Enterprise 1992.* ICC Publication no. 504. Oslo: Ad Notam Gyldendal.

World Commission on Environment and Development. 1987. *Our Common Future.* Oxford and New York: Oxford University Press.

Index

About the Authors

JOHN LUND HANSEN is Director of Consens A/S, Norway. He is a psychologist and management consultant.

PER A. CHRISTENSEN is Chief Executive, ODC Organisational Consultants Limited. He has consulted to businesses throughout the world.

The two have published books and articles on management and productivity, organizational change, and ecology.

ISBN 0-89930-916-X